Ribbon of Redemption

*True Stories Offering Hope And Healing
After Abortion*

Jenny A. Farrell

Scripture quotations marked (ESV) are from The Holy Bible,
English Standard Version, copyright 2001 by Crossway Bibles, a
publishing ministry of Good News Publishing. Used by
permission. All rights reserved.

Scripture quotations marked (NLT) are taken from The Holy Bible,
New Living Translation, copyright 1996, 2004, 2007, by Tyndale
House Foundation. Used by permission by Tyndale House
Publishers, Inc., Carol Stream, Illinois, 60188. All rights reserved.

Published in the United States by
Testimonies of Hope Publishing
PO Box 3951, Rock Island, IL 61204

Library of Congress Cataloging-in Publication Data

ISBN- 13: 978-0-9982090-0-5
ISBN- 10: 0-9982090-0-7

Acknowledgments

First and foremost, I will never cease to be grateful to each of you who entrusted your stories with me. Although you remain anonymous, it has taken tremendous courage to pull back the curtains from the windows of your souls. Be assured we will all be touched and changed because of your bravery.

Thank you, to Janice Boekhoff, Liz Ryan, Crystal Hoffman, Sheri Zeck and Bonnie Oberg, for taking me under your wings and patiently helping me along this writing path. I will be forever indebted to you all and look forward to future adventures together.

Charlie Farrell, you are not only the most wonderful husband any girl could have, but you are also my best friend. Thank you for being my biggest fan and for believing in me when I didn't believe in myself. I love you.

Brandon and Kelsey, you make this mama proud. You both have my heart.

Marsha Garrow, not only are you the best assistant anyone could ask for, but you are also a dear friend and accountability partner. Thank you for all you do.

Great appreciation goes to Kit Evans-Ford and the Testimonies of Hope Publishing team. You have given wings to my dream.

Finally, all praise and thanksgiving go to You, Father God. Every good gift comes from above, and I would not be able to write a single word without You. Thank You for the privilege to speak the truth in love.

~ Jenny

Order of Contents

Introduction

How long will it hurt?

I have written *Ribbon of Redemption* for two reasons. The first is to extend hope. If you are suffering from an abortion, or someone you love is struggling with a past abortion, I want you to know healing is available. As you read these intimate accounts, remember these are people just like yourself. At one point, they were filled with despair and hopelessness, yet now, they continue to discover new levels of healing and freedom.

Following each story, you will find a *Ribbon Reflection* and a *Going Deeper* section. These are designed to help you reflect on an aspect of that person's journey. Then go deeper, by seeing how their story might give insight into your own situation. This works in a small group setting as well as for individuals.

So why should I care?

I also wrote *Ribbon of Redemption* because abortion impacts every single person on the planet. Each day, we rub shoulders with people deeply affected by abortion. People just like you, who out of desperation took the "cure" offered. But instead of finding the relief they sought, their lives have been forever altered. For many, although their pregnancy ended, untold pain, grief, and shame took its place.

Prior to becoming a nurse at a life-affirming pregnancy center, abortion was simply a word. I was one of those people who held an opinion, yet hadn't truly delved into *why* I believed what I believed.

Now that I've been performing limited ultrasounds for the past ten years, these little lives have touched me deeply. Seeing a baby's heart beating as early as four weeks from conception demonstrates both to my patients and to me that this is indeed a *life*.

So what qualifies me to write this book? I have not personally experienced an abortion, yet after listening to hundreds of men and women scarred by abortion, I can no longer remain silent. I am a storyteller, and these brave men and women's stories deserve to be told.

Every year, we mourn the loss of nearly 3,000 American lives that were cut short on September 11, 2001. And so we should. But did you know that in the U.S. alone, there are over 3,000 babies aborted *every single day*? Or that 21% of all pregnancies in the U.S., excluding miscarriages, end in abortion? According to the Guttmacher Institute, since the Roe vs. Wade decision in 1973, there have been an estimated 58 million abortions.

As you read these accounts of lives nearly

destroyed, and the ripple effect that a *single* abortion has had on them and the ones they love, how could we ever begin to estimate the damage done to our nation by *58 million* abortions, and counting?

I chose the title *Ribbon of Redemption* because I believe each journey demonstrates how God can reach into the mess of our lives and transform it. Only He can take our tangled threads and weave something truly beautiful, even from the darkest strands.

My prayer is that you will be deeply touched, as I have been, by these journeys from tormented lives, to lives that have been redeemed. It's time for us to stop pointing fingers of blame and to start becoming part of the solution.

Together, we can make a difference, and demonstrate the love of Christ to a hurting world.

~Jenny

Mary's Story

Nothing about the day was right. It was beautiful, but that in itself was a betrayal. How could the sun be so calloused as to show its face on a day such as this?

Instead, the traitorous sky was a deep, azure blue. Trees edging the clearing were dressed in every shade of red, yellow and orange; the sunlight filtering through the collage of leaves like a beautiful patchwork of stained glass. The brilliant colors shone in sharp contrast with the black worn by those in attendance.

I couldn't look again. I knew better. Maybe if I just avoided the jarring image, I could still get through this. At least with my sunglasses firmly in place, no one could tell where my eyes were focused.

The man at the front was speaking words of comfort, reading from the book of Psalms, holding out hope. Still, when a heart is breaking, it takes time to heal.

Tears were expected on a day like today. But what if I lost control? I wasn't even part of the family.

How many years had it been since I broke down? Even cried just a little? I had become adept at keeping tears at bay, and this would not be the place to break my resolve. That would be far too great a risk.

Do what you do best, Mary. Take a deep breath and pull

yourself together.

That's when I made my fatal mistake. Eyes betraying me, I looked up toward the front, hearing the cries of the young girl. Why had they put her right in front of the box? Such a glossy, pearlescent white, with pretty silver accents. But knowing what the small rectangle contained made admiration for the workmanship impossible.

The pastor's voice finally stopped, and one by one the people filed up to the front. Some paused to gaze at the box once more, others hugged the young woman, gently leading her away.

At last, everyone was gone except the midwife, the grave digger, and myself. Staring at the tiny coffin, hovering over the gaping trench in the earth, I watched the midwife scoop up precious soil for the mother and put it in a jar—a remembrance of the brief life of her baby.

Why on earth had I agreed to give her a ride? Turning quickly away from the sad scene, it was as though I were truly taking in the rest of the cemetery for the first time. Wherever my glance rested, there were little markers dotting the earth; so many countless other tragedies on display.

The pressure was building inside my chest. Unable to catch a full breath, lava-like tears burned behind my eyelids, desperate for escape. Somehow, not one

11

spilled over.

Now, when finally free to escape, I found myself rooted to the ground, unable to move. Stomach clenching tightly, my body trembled. Finally, I lifted my eyes up toward the heavens, crying out inside my heart:

God, what am I doing here?

Abandoned

For years I wondered why my life had been spared—not once, but twice. From the moment I was born, life was a struggle. With weak, under-developed lungs, my first year was spent more in the hospital than out of it. My health became so precarious the doctor said unless I was moved to a warm, dry climate, I would never survive another Midwest winter.

My parents resisted at first, especially my mother. But after my doctor offered to pay our family's way, they finally agreed.

The day we began our train journey I was ill. Mother thought that if she waited for me to get well the day might never come. So with me in her arms and my two other brothers following close behind her, we boarded the train.

We had been on the train for many miles before the conductor discovered I was a very sick baby. Quickly, he found a physician on the train who took one look at me and whisked me away.

Mother said I was gone a while before the doctor returned. His news wasn't good. I was burning up with fever. Despite packing my body in ice, my temperature had soared to 106°, and I was convulsing. The doctor insisted Mother needed to get me to a hospital right away, or I would die.

But Mother refused to leave the train. She was completely overwhelmed. She only knew one thing; she had to get to my father as soon as possible. Besides, with very limited resources and not knowing a soul in the area, how would she be able to get me the help I needed?

So the doctor took charge and arranged for an ambulance to meet the train. They would transport me, my mother and brothers, to the nearest hospital in Tucson, Arizona. It was my only hope.

When the ambulance arrived, the attendants quickly assessed the situation and refused to take us. Our shabby clothing told them all they needed to know. *Who's going to pay for this? We're not running a charity!*

But once again, a physician fought to save my life. He insisted they would indeed take me with all haste to the hospital. He handed them money for the journey, with the promise of additional funds once he received word I had arrived safely. He also provided his private billing information, authorizing the hospital to do whatever they could for me at his expense.

What doctor would do such a thing? When I was older the Biblical story of the Good Samaritan became one of my favorites. It appeared that for some unknown reason, God very much wanted me to live.

~

The minute the ambulance made it to the hospital I was whisked to critical care with little hope offered. For two days my life hung in the balance, while Mother and the boys slept in chairs in the cramped waiting room.

Once Daddy finally arrived, the head doctor met with my parents. He was quite blunt. He suggested my family should leave me. Nothing could be done but to keep me comfortable. It was uncertain how long I would linger, but they assured my parents I would not survive. What should they do? For the betterment of the family, they got back on the train and headed to Phoenix.

On one level my rational mind could understand how my parents made such a drastic choice. My heart reacts differently. How does a parent leave their dying child? How does a mother walk away? In my mind's eye, I see a tiny baby girl on a bed too large for her. Big people are all around, poking and prodding. But she cries because the faces are unfamiliar.

All I knew was I had been left behind.

A week later, they received a startling phone call. Expecting to hear I had died, my parents learned I had made it through the worst of it and was steadily improving. Two weeks later my family once again boarded a train to Phoenix. This time, I was with them.

~

The constant Arizona sunshine and lack of humidity proved to be a wonderful combination for me. Just as a healthy plant thrives on sunlight, apparently so did I. With fresh air and daily doses of sunshine, I was soon running around like any other active toddler.

We remained in Arizona for ten years. During that time Mother gave birth to three more sons. With six children to feed, money was tight. Daddy worked hard but could not adequately provide for us. Abandoned by his family for choosing a wife outside the Amish community, he was shunned. Coupled with having a limited education, Dad had a difficult time securing a good job. To make ends meet, Mom went to work as a certified nurse's aide.

The appearance of faith was important, or maybe it was something we just did. During the early years, we all attended church together. Somehow, though, the message of love and belonging never seemed to penetrate our lives. Resentment colored my mother's world and consequently mine as well.

At the time, I didn't understand all Mom gave up when we moved to Arizona. Other than her husband and children, she left everything that was familiar. Some people can adapt to such a drastic change, but my mother wasn't one of them. For her, it was crippling.

Mom's resentment echoed through every aspect of my life. I craved her approval, but when things got difficult Mom would throw my illness in my face. *If you weren't so sickly, we wouldn't have needed to come here in the first place!* I heard those words over and over. They cut deep, creating a wound that would fester for years.

Approval

When I was in the sixth grade, we returned to Illinois. I struggled with respiratory infections, but thankfully, I rarely missed school. By the time I was in eighth grade, I had nearly outgrown my tendency towards pneumonia. I was stronger.

Having five brothers predisposed me to be a tomboy. Despite my health issues, I had always been a determined little girl. I was just as good as anyone else, including boys. Maybe even better. Thankfully, my brothers never babied me, and through the years I was always included in the baseball and football games which were played on a daily basis.

Sports was something I both loved and excelled in. When deciding on a career, it made sense to pursue a degree in education, with the goal of becoming a high school coach.

Mom was pleased since it was very important to her that we all go to college and have careers. She struggled with my father's lack of even a high school diploma, and his consequent inability to earn a good wage. She wanted more for her children.

The first year I was at the university my maternal grandmother died quite suddenly of a massive stroke. I could hardly believe it. For the first time, I had to deal with the loss of someone who was very precious to me. Grandma had loved me unconditionally. I had never even considered the world without her in it. It was as though an earthquake had hit our family, and I was left surrounded by rubble.

If Grandma's death was traumatic for the rest of us, it affected Mom far more. She struggled during the next couple of years, spending more and more time working at the hospital.

I lived in the dorms at college but came home on the occasional weekend. I began noticing Mom becoming increasingly more irritable with Dad, but I chalked it up to Grandmother's death. Still, her resentment was quite obvious.

Why couldn't she see how exhausted he was, trying to meet the needs of our family? He worked extremely hard at the local steel mill. It wasn't easy. Nearly every night his arms were burned from carrying the hot, galvanized steel. He spent numerous hours of overtime at the Mill, to ensure all his children attended college. I tried to encourage Mom to go easy on Dad. But it was obvious the toll it was taking on my father.

~

In my final year of college, I met Tom. He was a wonderful guy—there was just something about him that drew me in. But I couldn't afford to be distracted. I was just finishing my student teaching, as well as handling my heavy academic load. I had to stay focused.

Still, Tom was persistent, making his interest clear. He contented himself with the occasional phone call, eventually letting me know he was willing to wait for me as long as it took. Occasionally, after a long day, I would return to the dorm to find a beautiful bouquet of flowers waiting for me. Tom was definitely making points.

When graduation day arrived, Tom was there along with my family. Everyone liked him and got along well, even if my brothers enjoyed giving him a hard time. It was all in good fun. What a perfect day to have the people I most cared about there to celebrate my achievement. I had a substitute teaching position in town that would begin in a couple of months so I would be living back home for the year. In the meantime, Tom and I began to make the most of our time together.

~

One day I came home from teaching and found Mom and Dad fighting. When I asked what was going on, Mom informed me she was filing for divorce.

At first, I was sure she was kidding, even if it was a terrible joke. But I saw the set of her jaw and the narrowing of her eyes. She was absolutely serious.

The shock was like someone had punched me in the gut. What in the world was going on?

Daddy walked out of the room, a look of defeat on his face. I tried to talk some sense into Mom, but she was determined. She claimed she had never really loved Dad—it was time for *her* to be happy.

The boxing match continued, and I was about to get knocked out. I didn't see it coming. She told me she'd been having an affair with a woman from work for some time. The woman also planned to file for divorce, and they intended to move in together to start a new life.

In a single moment, the axis of my world suddenly tilted, and everything I held dear began sliding at a rapid pace towards the cliff of uncertainty. I shook my head, trying to clear it. This couldn't be happening.

What about my father? He had walked away from his family and his Amish roots to spend his life with my mother. Now, she was walking out on him, making a mockery of their life together and of his love.

Then in the midst of the divorce, the other woman's husband stepped in, putting an end to the relationship and cutting off all contact between them. Mom had already filed for divorce and had said things that could never be taken back. She continued with the divorce proceedings, but instead of moving out she remained under the same roof as my father. Talk about confusing.

I stood by helplessly, watching my dad close himself off. It was obvious he was in pain, but I didn't know how to reach him. I knew he was incapable of navigating such treacherous waters, but so was I. My siblings were suffering too, but I didn't know what to do for them.

My mother became quite depressed. With all her plans falling apart, she withdrew from everyone. I came home from work one day and found her on the floor unresponsive. Having swallowed a bottle of pills, she needed her stomach pumped. What was I to do? I couldn't be with her night and day, nor did I want to. I was angry for all she was putting my father through.

My heart was filled with gratitude for Tom during that time. He was my rock of reason when nothing else made sense. He turned out to be very caring and instinctively knew what I needed, even when I had no clue. We were falling in love. Lonely and confused, seeking solace, I turned to Tom for comfort, and for the first time we became intimate.

Mom made another suicide attempt, only this time she very nearly succeeded. According to the attending doctor at the ER it was a miracle that she had survived. She voluntarily committed herself to an inpatient mental health facility. Once she was released, I could see it had made a difference. She seemed more at peace with herself.

Growing up, Mom had always been reticent to share details about her past. But one day, out of the blue, she revealed she was the product of an affair. Later, her mother had married her stepfather, and the fact that Mom was not his child became common knowledge. Despite being the oldest sibling, she was treated like an outcast by her brothers and sisters. Far worse, her stepfather had repeatedly beaten and molested her for years.

Hearing her story made me want to empathize with her. What a terrible thing to have endured. No wonder she was so broken.

But how did I offer grace when my own heart was so bitter? Her attempt to gain my sympathy fell short. The way my mother had treated Dad was inexcusable, and resentment, even rage, had been building for months. She may have wanted compassion for her difficult life, but that was something I did not have to give.

A Choice

Then, I got a real break. One of the high schools where I had once substituted called, offering a full-time, permanent position. Not only would I teach Health and Physical Education, but I would also be the women's head varsity coach. Quickly agreeing, I did a happy dance. Things were looking up.

~

The next day I realized I had not had a period in two months. I'd been so busy with all that was happening I simply hadn't been paying attention. How could I have been so stupid? Suddenly, my physical symptoms added up. I was pregnant.

No! This had to be a mistake. Not like this. Not now, when everything I'd worked so hard for was about to come true. A baby would be impossible at this point in my life.

I wasn't sure how Dad would react to the news, but there was no question in my mind what Mom would say. How many times had I heard her ridicule single women whose babies she cared for at the nursery? *They should have just aborted! The baby doesn't even have a chance at a real life.*

Tom was in shock when he heard the news. Raised in a very conservative home, he knew his parents would see a pregnancy outside of marriage as

24

almost unforgivable. Even if we got married right away, the math wouldn't have added up.

After going back and forth for a while, Tom got the number of an abortion clinic, and with my full agreement, made an appointment for later that week.

The clinic looked like a storefront, but without the presence of other businesses. Chairs lined the room, filled with women and a handful of men. Tom was sent on an errand to purchase supplies for the ride home.

When my name was called to officially check in, they wanted immediate payment in full. I felt so foolish. Why didn't I think to ask Tom for the money before he left? There was zero negotiating—full payment had to be received immediately in order to secure my appointment. Since there was no way to reach Tom, I was informed I would now have to be the last case of the day.

The waiting was difficult. I had brought nothing to read or do. Nothing to distract myself from the thoughts of what lay ahead. The silence was deafening. Even though the room was packed, not an idle word was spoken. The only sound that occasionally shattered the stillness was when the next woman was called back. The noise caused all eyes to turn, watching as she followed the worker back.

When Tom returned, he immediately apologized for not thinking about leaving the cash. For hours, the two of us sat waiting in the unnatural stillness.

Finally, my name was called, but I wished it was for anything else than to have an abortion. I didn't *want* an abortion. It just seemed the only possible answer to an impossible situation. A door I thought I had to walk through.

Without preamble, I was taken straight to a surgical room and told to remove my clothing. There was no explanation of the procedure nor any time allowed for questions. I was instructed to lay on the table and to cover up with the sheet provided. That was the extent of my preparation for what was to come.

When the abortionist walked in, he sat down without saying a word. There was the sound of clanging metal, then a horrendous pain sliced through me, as though all of my insides were bring ripped from my body. I wasn't given any anesthesia or pain medicine. I tried to distract myself; to focus on the nurse beside me. But there was no way to block out the sensations overwhelming every cell in my body.

Lifting my head, I craned my neck trying to see what could be causing such horrific pain. I saw the glint of surgical steel and watched it disappear beneath the sheet. The pain was beyond anything I could have ever imagined. I never dreamt the procedure would feel as though I were being raped by metal instruments. It seemed to go on forever.

Finally, it was over. As I got off the table, I had the oddest sensation of being disconnected from my body—as though I wasn't even sure how to operate it.

Led to a room full of army cots, I was told to lie down and be still. Several other women were there, but once again, an eerie silence permeated the area, except for an occasional sound of whimpering.

Eventually, a woman in scrubs came over and asked if I was "okay." Once I nodded, that was it. I got up on shaky legs and walked out. No instructions. Nothing as to what to expect, or what would be considered an emergency.

The drive back with Tom continued in silence. Neither of us referred to the abortion. We acted like nothing unusual had happened. He dropped me off at my house and continued to his place. Each of us acting oblivious of what had just happened.

After that, I tried to resume life as though nothing had changed. But when I was alone, I couldn't deny that something was very wrong. It felt as though I had just been sexually assaulted, only worse. The memory of both the physical and emotional pain never left me. Somehow, I wasn't able to put the two traumas together; it was as if they existed on two separate planes.

Part of me longed to tell someone. But who? Mom was wrapped up in her haze of pain. Was she even capable of understanding how traumatic it had all been? Who else could I trust with something this painful? This shameful?

It would be years before I told another soul.

Achieve

Attempting to move on with my life, I behaved as though nothing had happened. No matter how hard I tried, the abortion was never far from my mind. There was a pervasive sense that something was desperately wrong, though exactly what was unclear. But there was no going back. What was done was done, and somehow, I had to move on.

~

I started my new teaching position in a small community an hour from my hometown. I was kept incredibly busy, which was a good thing. I truly enjoyed my new job, yet it seemed like somehow my "mute button" was on. Laughter and excitement were a rare thing. Still, I loved interacting with the young women and watching them grow.

Tom and I continued to see each other as often as we could, and the following year I moved closer to home. A few months later we were married.

My first two pregnancies ended in an early miscarriage. I remember almost nothing about either one. I never cried a single tear. It was as though I were frozen.

I couldn't allow myself to feel the loss, let alone mourn for my babies. If I started, I might never be able to stop. I was numb, as though the anesthesia I

29

had never received during my abortion was somehow administered to my emotions instead.

There was also a secret fear that I kept completely hidden: What if I was like Mom? What if I totally lost my mind?

After accepting a full-time position at the local Catholic high school, I found myself immediately drawn to Sister Mary. Something about her demeanor told me I could trust her with anything.

Several months later, I finally found the courage to let my guard down. I told Sister Mary, who listened intently to my story without interruption. Sensing no judgment, that alone brought a level of healing to my soul.

Although I had given my heart to God when I was young, after the abortion it was as though a distance sprang up between us. On one level, I believed God had forgiven me the moment I had repented. I knew He would never abandon me.

But how could I truly accept that forgiveness? Even more, how could I ever forgive myself? I had grievously sinned when I sacrificed the life of my child, and I had erected a wall with the stones of shame, guilt, and fear. A wall so thick and so tall that it seemed to shut out God's love and light.

God never left me. But the wall I had believed would

serve as my protection, limited my ability to access His love and forgiveness fully.

~

Tom and I were delighted when I delivered a baby boy later that year. We named him Jeremiah. He was such a precious little guy, and we both loved him dearly. At times I would be seized with an irrational fear that something terrible would happen to him, but I pushed it down. I was an expert at doing that. Out of sight, out of mind.

After four years, I accepted another teaching position in a neighboring town. I still needed much healing, but I would always be grateful for Sister Mary's love and grace in my life.

~

Jeremiah was three months old when I began my new job as the Physical Education Director and the coach of women's volleyball and track. I remained at the school for several years and loved it. In addition to my regular duties, I always seemed to end up listening to a student who was going through a difficult time. It was my way of giving to them what I had once longed for as a teenager.

After a few years, I was approached with an offer of a new position as Director of Student Activities. I never thought of myself as a counselor, but the idea intrigued me. However, to officially meet with students in a way I had already be doing for years, I would need to get my master's in counseling. It was a huge decision. With both full-time work and full-time school, who would care for Jeremiah?

After praying, Tom and I agreed this was what the Lord had planned for me. My husband did the lion share of caring for our son, while I spent hours poring over books as well as working one on one with the students. It was exhausting, but I loved every minute of it.

Redemption

Several years later, as a high school counselor, I had been helping a teenage girl, named Beth, through an unplanned pregnancy. A few weeks from her due date Beth experienced complications. After hours of labor she delivered a beautiful little girl, who never took her first breath.

Later that day, the whole school knew about the tragedy. Almost immediately it was as though everyone went into mourning. Teachers and students alike were experiencing much sadness and confusion. I was grateful Beth had a good support system around her, but knew I needed to attend the funeral to show that I deeply cared.

A few days later, as I entered the sanctuary, my eyes were riveted to a tiny white casket up at the front of the room. Such a glossy, pearlescent white, with intricate silver accents. But the lid was closed, and knowing of the small form that lay within it, nothing about the box was attractive.

Something like a jolt of electricity hit me, even as my chest tightened. Finding it hard to take a deep breath, I quickly slipped into one of the empty seats. What was the matter with me? Had I imagined there could be a funeral without a casket?

But there was nothing ordinary about the casket— nothing ordinary about any of it. I just needed to get through the service and get out of there as quickly as possible.

I felt a tap on my shoulder. Turning around, inwardly I cringed, although attempting to return the smile. It was Susan Thompson, the mother of one of my former track students, who had slipped in behind me. Was she going to talk to me here? Now?

I remembered Susan as a bit flamboyant—an extrovert. Leaning forward, till her mouth was mere inches from my face, she started whispering loudly. Did I know that she had been the midwife taking care of Beth and the baby? Such a sad case.

I wanted to clamp my hands over my ears and disappear into the carpet. By now, people had begun to stare. That was the last thing I wanted. So, I gave her my most polite this-is-the-end-of-the-conversation smile and turned back, facing the front.

During the service, I felt bad, but I tuned the preacher out entirely, trying to distract myself with all the things I needed to do the rest of the week. I had to get through this in one piece, and I was sure the words in the sermon wouldn't help me do that. Just being at the service alone was stirring up the ghosts of memories best left forgotten.

After the service, I was trying to get to my car as quickly as possible, without being rude, when Susan caught up with me. Would I mind giving her a ride to the graveside service? Apparently, the people she'd ridden with had decided against going to the cemetery.

I heard myself agreeing, even as I led her out to my car. Why was I such a pushover? Why couldn't I have come up with a good excuse for not being able to help her?

Before I'd even put the key in the ignition, Susan began talking again, this time even sharing details about the difficult delivery and how tragic it was. So much for HIPPA regulations. Head beginning to pound, I told myself I would insist we leave as fast as we could. I couldn't wait to put the nightmare behind me.

But there would be no quick getaway. On top of everything else, Susan said she'd promised Beth she would collect a little dirt from the gravesite for a memory. We wouldn't be able to do that until everyone else left. I didn't mind a few extra minutes, did I?

What could I say? So I simply nodded and as soon as the car was in park I walked to the far edge of the trees, away from the open tent with the neat rows of chairs already filled with family. Beth had cried throughout the funeral, and I wished I had been able to go over and offer her some comfort. But I knew I needed to keep my distance.

What an awful day. It was beautiful, but that in itself seemed a betrayal. How could the sun be shining when our hearts felt so dark? There should have at least been clouds.

Thankfully, I had grabbed my sunglasses from the car before stepping out. At least I had something to hide behind. The preacher opened his Bible and began talking. Again, I assumed he would speak some words designed to comfort, but I didn't dare focus in that direction. I couldn't look at the tiny coffin again. Maybe if I just avoided the jarring image, pretending to listen, I could get through this without breaking down.

Tears were expected on a day like today—but what if I totally lost it? I was the school counselor—the one who was supposed to help everyone else in a crisis, not the other way around.

I'd become adept at keeping tears at bay. How many years had it been since I broke down? Even shed a tear? That was a risk I was unwilling to take.

Finally, the pastor's voice stopped, and one by one people began to scatter. Some walked over to gaze at the sad little casket once more. Others hugged Beth, her family gently leading her away.

At last, everyone else was gone, except Susan, the grave digger, and myself. I couldn't seem to avoid the sight of the tiny coffin any longer, hovering over the gaping trench in the earth. I watched as Susan gently scooped up the dirt, placing it in the small jar. A gesture to preserve a tangible memory of the brief life of her baby.

Then the thought struck, like a lightning bolt across my mind. What tangible memory did I have of *my* first baby? In a flash, I was back in that room. Could hear the clink of the metal instruments of death, feel the pain and the emptiness.

What had they done with my baby? My miscarriages had occurred very early in my pregnancies. But how far along had I been with my first? Twelve weeks? Far enough that everything was already intricately formed—a tiny replica of a full-sized baby, just needing time to grow. Time I hadn't been willing to give.

My heart burned within, as though the sun had scorched it, exposing it as a fraud. Pulling my eyes away from the mournful scene, I glanced around. There were so many little markers dotting the earth; countless other tragedies on display.

Suddenly, pressure built inside my chest. I couldn't catch a full breath, even as lava-like tears banked behind my eyelids, desperately needing an escape.

Now, when I was finally about to leave, I found myself rooted to the ground, unable to move. Stomach clenching tightly, my body trembled.

Finally, I lifted my eyes up toward the heavens, crying out inside my heart: *God, what am I doing here?*

Into the stillness, I heard God's voice: *It's time to begin grieving your aborted baby.*

I was stunned, but the message resonated within the core of my being. It was time. Time to finally look at what I had been unable to acknowledge for a very, very long time.

~

Later that day, I called a trusted friend, asking if she knew of any place that helped someone dealing with a past abortion. She told me about Rachel's Vineyard. It was a weekend retreat program focused on post-abortion healing.

That night, I told Tom what had happened to me. Told him about how difficult it had all been. How I was totally out of my element.

Other than years before when Tom shared his vision of seeing our son in heaven, this was the first time we had ever spoken about our abortion in twenty-seven years.

Tom broke down when he saw the pain reflected in my eyes. I had hidden it for so long, not wanting to burden him with my grief. But gradually his tortuous journey emerged. How he had agonized even while he sat in that waiting room so long ago, wishing he'd had the courage to jump up and take me out of that awful place. How he'd endured many dreams where he had woken up crying, the threads of the dream gone, and only the acute pain of tremendous loss remaining.

I told him about the Rachel's Vineyard retreats and how I wanted to book a weekend for the two us as soon as possible.

At first, he was more than a little resistant. He was sure he would be the only man there. How would a bunch of women crying be of any help to him? But eventually he reluctantly agreed, and I immediately signed us both up.

The day of the retreat arrived, and we were both filled with apprehension. What would it be like? Who else would be there? At the same time, I was also excited about the prospect of finding even a small measure of freedom from the guilt and shame that I had carried for so long.

Halfway to our destination, Tom proposed that we spend a romantic weekend in a nearby city instead of going to the retreat. We could do whatever I chose. We could even talk about the abortion if I wanted to, he just didn't want to talk about it in front of a bunch of strangers.

My heart went out to him. I identified with his fear more than he knew. But I also wanted the healing I desperately hoped was coming. God had led us to this point, and He wouldn't abandon us now.

I gently told him I *had* to go. That we had to face this together. Finally, once again he reluctantly agreed.

It took a few hours to get there, but it was a beautiful drive. What a contrast between the drive we had taken twenty-seven years before and the one we were now on. Instead of driving towards death, we were moving towards healing and wholeness. Despite our mutual anxiety of the unknown, there was no comparison to the silent dread we had both experienced on the way to that clinic.

Walking up to the retreat house, the sight of yellow roses along the walkway was like a sweet message from the Lord. Seeing my favorite flowers was a reassurance that we were indeed on the right path.

We were greeted warmly by Dr. Theresa Burke, who we later learned was the founder of Rachel's Vineyard. What a genuine person who completely emanated the love of Christ!

Tom was pleasantly surprised when he learned there were four other couples there. He wouldn't be the only man. Also, the priest who was there would play a large role in helping Tom find a measure of comfort.

Part of the biggest opportunity for healing occurred on the final day. We were instructed to write a letter to our aborted child/children. When it was time for me to read mine aloud, I found I was unable to read more than a few words before I broke down. Tears poured out, turning into sobs. It was the very first time I had cried in the twenty-seven years since my abortion.

In the presence of such warmth and acceptance, it was as if a frozen river had thawed, causing the dam to break and the water to overflow its banks. But in the atmosphere of love and compassion, my emotions weren't as frightening as they once were. I began to experience the cleansing and healing properties of tears. They became a balm to my soul, washing away the debris of self-hatred, guilt and shame.

In addition to the letters to our aborted or miscarried children, we had been instructed to write a letter to our "inner child." Over the past few days, I had learned we all had deeply wounded parts of ourselves we had shut away, unable to acknowledge due to the painful memories attached to them.

In my letter, I apologized to my "inner child" for shutting her out of my life—for not letting her express the grief that had been bottled up for so long. It was such a freeing and cleansing experience.

Before we even left, I knew that Tom and I needed to be part of such a wonderful and necessary effort. I longed to help others find wholeness and healing from the pain of abortion. We were part of Rachel's Vineyard Ministries for several years. Eventually, I became the counselor for many future retreats.

I will be forever grateful to those who served us on our weekend. I had been like a shadow for so long, cut off from vital parts of myself. The Lord used those loving and compassionate men and women to administer Christ's love to my wounded soul—helped me face the fear, the guilt, and the shame. With their support, I was able to experience healthy repentance and to receive Christ's forgiveness, as well as to begin to forgive myself.

~

One evening, I heard an advertisement on the radio. It was for an executive director position at one of the local life-affirming pregnancy centers. Instantly, I sensed in my spirit that I was to apply for the job.

There were several obstacles. One, I had never worked in the capacity of an executive director before. Two, it would mean I would have to give up my significant teaching retirement which was nearly funded. It would also mean a huge loss in salary.

But I had been learning that those things were nothing in comparison with the joy of obeying and pleasing my God. He was calling me, and I would listen.

I quickly applied for the position and wasn't surprised when I received the call telling me the job was mine. That very week I began serving women and men facing an unplanned pregnancy. Also, I continued to minister to those who suffered from the heartache of a past abortion. I've been serving at the Center for over eight years now and have loved every moment of it.

I will always regret my abortion. I long to see my child in heaven, and to hold him in my arms. To this day the sound of clinking metal in the doctor's office can take me back to that abortion room. But it's temporary. I know what to do with those feelings of guilt and shame. Jesus died on a cruel cross and paid the debt for my sin. I have been forgiven! And I have forgiven those who lied to me or wounded me as well.

Sometimes, I wonder how I ever walked through those doors. Why hadn't I listened to the Lord and found a different solution? I am still facing consequences because of that decision. I endured much heartache for years, and there will always be someone missing from our family.

My parents are both gone now. Dad lived to the ripe old age of eighty-six, having learned to love God with all his heart. Once my youngest brother was out of the house, my father moved to Oklahoma where his family lived. He never joined the Amish church, but reconciled with his family and the community, so the elders lifted the Bann.

My mother struggled throughout her life. Although she knew about God's love, she was never able to fully receive the healing available to her here on Earth. Echoes of her abuse still haunted her.

Our relationship continued to be strained. In my head, I knew my mother loved me, yet in many ways, her actions denied that.

In the final days of her life, she was slipping in and out of consciousness. Even when she was awake, we never knew when she would have a lucid moment. They had become rare, due to a brain tumor. But one day she looked at me and spoke with perfect clarity. *You do know that I love you?*

As the tears coursed down my cheeks, I understood my hunger to hear those three words. *I love you.*

~

I marvel at how God is now using me to help others. By speaking the truth in love, and by providing a window to see their child through ultrasound, many have made a choice about their pregnancy that they can feel good about. I also continue to minister to those wounded by abortion.

In addition, I have been blessed beyond my wildest dreams with a husband who still adores me and with my son Jeremiah, who has grown into a remarkable young man.

The Bible says the one who has been forgiven much, loves much. That certainly applies to me. I am astounded at God's amazing grace and mercy extended to me, and long to see others freed from their chains as well.

What if those of us who have been set free from the bondage of abortion were to reach out and help others? I believe if we all did our part, we would witness a huge healing occur throughout our nation, as well as literally around the world.

"You have kept count of my tossings, put my tears in Your bottle, are they not in Your book? Then my enemies will turn back in the day when I call. This I know, that God is for me."

Psalm 56:8-9 (ESV)

Ribbon Reflection

One of the threads of Mary's story that struck me deeply was how she suppressed her emotions. I was stunned when she told me she had not shed a single tear in the twenty-seven years since her abortion.

Unfortunately, hers is not an isolated case.

I recall a beautiful young woman who came to our center for a pregnancy test. We'll call her Maria. The result turned out to be negative, but while taking her health history, she admitted to having had an abortion about two years previously. Finding herself somewhere safe that day, and not sensing judgment, she began sharing her experience.

Mary and Maria had something in common. Mary was about to launch into her career, while this young woman was due to begin university with a full-ride scholarship. She didn't want anything to get in the way of her dream, so without telling even the father of the baby, she immediately obtained an abortion.

Maria went on to college in the fall, as planned, and excelled academically. She was where she had always wanted to be. But something was very wrong.

Living in the dorms was always part of the dream — experiencing "campus life." Now, none of that mattered anymore. In fact, she found herself avoiding her fellow classmates as much as possible, preferring to remain alone.

I noticed that as the interview continued, Maria used a phrase quite frequently. When she told me that her so called "best friend" got angry with her and posted on Facebook that she'd had an abortion, I was appalled. Knowing how painful that must have been, I expressed how sorry I was that she had suffered such a betrayal.

Her response? "It doesn't matter," with an accompanying dismissive flick of her hand.

Finally, I asked her, "You say "it doesn't matter" frequently.

Does *anything* matter to you? Maria just paused, looking at me.

"No. Nothing matters anymore. Nothing at all."

She went on to say that since the abortion, she never laughed or cried. It was best to live in the safety zone of blunted emotions; avoiding all highs and lows. Those meant the possibility of losing control, something that had to be avoided at all costs.

What about you? Have you experienced an abortion, and now you're tiptoeing around life, trying not to wake the sleeping giant? Or perhaps you're dealing with a past abuse, or another secret, that is tearing you up inside.

I strongly encourage you to check out the section at the back of the book called, "Where Do I Go from Here?" There are places you can call and speak confidentially with someone who cares about you— finally ending the silence. Healing will take time, but rest assured, the God of all comfort longs to see you set free.

And so do I.

Going Deeper

1. Mary's story as a baby is so remarkable. To have two different doctors fighting to save her life, to the point of paying great sums of money so that she would have a chance to live.

    a. Think back over your own lifetime and share about a time when someone showed you a kindness that helped you survive a difficult season.

    b. As you look back, in the midst of the struggle and the pain, can you trace a thread which reveals God is *for* you?

2. Whether you know it yet or not, you have an enemy. John 10:10 says. "The thief comes only to steal, kill and destroy. I came that they may have life, and have it abundantly." (ESV) Looking at Mary's life, identify ways it is evident that someone is trying to "steal, kill and destroy" her.

3. Mary believed she had to keep a tight lid on her emotions or she might crack wide open. Maybe even lose her sanity.

    a. Can you recall a time in your life when you were afraid to laugh or cry? What helped you get through that time?

    b. If you are still in that place of "blunted emotions," can you identify what helped Mary face her pain and begin to heal?

4. Psalm 56 is one of my favorite chapters in the Bible. I love verses 8-9. Something about knowing that God cares about my pain and tears is extremely comforting to me.

   a. Read the verses aloud, listed just prior to *Going Deeper*. How does the fact that God loves you enough to keep track of the pain and confusion you experience impact you?

   b. What does verse 9 mean to you when it says that God is *for* you?

Tom's Story

(Mary's Husband)

Control

I always knew one day I would be a husband and a father. In that order—wedding first, babies second. I made a commitment to myself and to God to remain sexually pure until I was married.

I practically grew up in the church. Hearing Bible stories come alive on Sunday mornings was something I looked forward to. At a young age, I gave my heart to Jesus.

When I was a senior in high school, my fifteen-year-old sister, Jill, got pregnant. I will never forget my father's reaction the day he discovered her condition. He treated her as though she were something vile: "No daughter of mine will be seen pregnant around here!"

So Jill was packed up and sent off to a maternity home for unwed mothers in another state. After that, it was as if a dark cloud descended on our home, contaminating the atmosphere.

Once Jill gave birth, her baby was taken and placed for immediate adoption.

I certainly have nothing against adoption; quite the opposite. I think adoption is a beautiful thing and a wonderful option. What bothered me terribly was the way Jill had been treated, forcibly removing the little boy from her, even though she desperately wanted to keep him.

Even after Jill returned home, my father continued to treat her with utter disdain, using silence as a means to continue her punishment.

I always felt things deeply. Not simply my own responses to what was going on, but often the pain others were experiencing. Watching Jill sink further into hopelessness and despair nearly broke my heart. It also made me extremely angry.

Although I still loved God and wanted to follow Him, I was left with much confusion. How could the man who taught me about God and took me to church, turn around and treat his own daughter the way he did? And why hadn't I tried harder to protect her?

From that moment on, I determined my father would never wield that kind of control in my life. Under no circumstances would I give him the opportunity to destroy me, like he nearly destroyed my sister.

Broken

I had been on my own for several years when I met Mary. Immediately, I was drawn to her. She was not only beautiful, but strong, confident, and compassionate.

She was also a challenge.

When I first asked her out, the timing was off. At least that's what she told me. She was in the middle of her last year of college and was student teaching as well. She said she didn't have time to date. But when I persisted, she agreed to talk to me as often as she could by phone. Occasionally I would also send her flowers. I wanted her to know how special she was, and I definitely didn't want her to forget me and set her sights on anyone else.

By the time we had our first official date I knew she was the one for me. I was head-over-heels in love with her.

We tried to be careful. To try to spend most of our time together in public places. But we were in love and temptation got the best of us. We became lovers.

I knew we were playing with fire, but nothing could have prepared me for the moment I heard the words "I'm pregnant." In a flash, all the fears I had as a teenager came rushing back. Now I was the one with the unplanned pregnancy. I wasn't fifteen, but would my father see it any differently? As the oldest boy, I had always been held to an even higher standard than my siblings.

I worried about Mary too. She was just about to begin her career as a teacher and athletic director. She'd worked hard and long to get where she was, and having a baby at that point just didn't make sense.

For weeks, I agonized over what we should do. I had been at my job for about seven years and had done very well for myself. But during those couple of weeks I was so distraught I made some mistakes and was nearly fired.

That's when I confided my situation to my supervisor. He was a few years older than me, and I had always looked up to him. He took the time to listen; then he shared that he and his girlfriend had found themselves in a similar situation, and she had chosen to have an abortion. According to him, it was quick, and there was "nothing to it." He even gave me his phone number if I needed to talk further.

I was blown away. I could never have talked to my dad like that. He seemed to genuinely care about me, so I took his advice seriously.

It's not as though the option of abortion had not been brought up. I had also confided in a couple of friends who agreed abortion seemed the best choice.

We should "just take care of it and live our lives."

That evening, Mary and I sat down together and made the final decision to abort. With her consent, I dialed the number my boss had given me, setting an appointment for two days later.

The next thing I knew, Mary and I were in the waiting room of an abortion clinic. We sat there holding hands as she waited for her name to be called. Despite the room being full of people, it was totally silent.

The silence must have been contagious because Mary and I didn't say a word either. We just sat there mute, watching the hands on the clock creep around the face of the dial. All I had were my thoughts, and those were in a complete jumble.

Deep down I knew we shouldn't be there. I desperately wanted the courage to speak up. *To heck with what my father says or does! Let's get married and start our family.*

But I said nothing.

When Mary's name was finally called, she stood up, turned to flash a little smile my way, and disappeared behind the closed door.

I waited for what seemed like an eternity, while I worried about what the abortion might do to Mary. I continued to berate myself for not walking out of the clinic while we still had the chance.

In my mind, I saw myself getting up and storming through the door to find Mary, whisking her away from that place of death. But once the pictures in my head were gone I was still sitting squarely on the chair in the waiting room. I had done nothing.

When Mary finally came out, she smiled at me and took my hand.

I don't know what I expected. She seemed a little tired, but not in extreme pain or traumatized. Maybe everything was going to be okay.

So I stuffed my own feelings down into a dark well, trying to forget what we had done.

When?

Mary and I continued to talk frequently, seeing each other as often as our schedules allowed. Within a year, I was standing at the front of the church as I watched the woman I loved walk towards me with a bouquet of flowers in her hands. Soon the pastor was saying "you may kiss the bride."

It was a beautiful ceremony, and I was thrilled Mary was finally my wife. But just like everything else, it was as though a darkness hung like a shroud over our day. I couldn't escape the fact that our baby was missing.

Over the years, my love for Mary only deepened. The one area I knew she struggled with was the miscarriages. I would delight over a positive pregnancy test, only to later grieve when the doctors said she was in the process of losing the baby.

But even then, Mary appeared to handle the losses with such strength. Nothing seemed to hold her back or keep her down. She always bounced back quickly and began focusing on the next goal.

Sometimes, in the middle of the night, I would startle awake, my face wet with tears. Instantly, I would know I had dreamt about our baby, but as hard as I tried, I could never remember a single detail. It was as though I immediately had amnesia, yet it always evoked such a deep longing—an emptiness impossible to fill.

I desperately wanted to wake Mary and tell her everything. But I never did. Why should I cause her pain, just to make myself feel better? She seemed to be doing okay. I didn't want to heap guilt on her... that was mine to bear.

I would lay in the dark, plagued with guilt and shame. I longed to have those moments back. Sitting in the waiting room that day, I hadn't used the time the way I should have. God had given me the opportunity to make it right. Why hadn't I had the courage to do what I wanted to do? Why hadn't I stepped up and been the man God created me to be?

I couldn't escape the truth that we would probably have a child to love, instead of a child we missed desperately, if only Mary had known I would be there for both her and the baby.

If I could have gone back in time and changed my decision, there would have been zero hesitation. I would've done my best to see that Mary and I ran out of that clinic—and never looked back.

~

A couple of years later, we were excited when we purchased tickets to a concert for our favorite Christian band. The band was called Harvest, and one of the reasons we liked them was because they tackled tough subjects the church was facing, but rarely spoke about.

We were standing together, enjoying the music, when they played a new song that hit me at the core of my being. It was about abortion, and suddenly all the feelings came rushing to the surface.

Near the end of the concert the leader gave an opportunity for anyone who wanted to give their life to Christ, or to rededicate their life, to come down front. Mary and I had been holding hands, and we both squeezed the other's at the same moment. Looking into her eyes, I knew exactly what she wanted. We would respond to the invitation together.

Weaving our way down to the stage, we ended up standing in front of one of the huge speakers as the band continued to sing another song, giving others a chance to get to the front. The deep notes of the bass coming out of the speakers was so intense it made my body vibrate.

Still holding Mary's hand, I closed my eyes and began crying out to God—begging Him to forgive me for ending my child's life.

Suddenly, I felt myself being drawn quickly away, the music gradually growing softer, until it disappeared altogether.

Then I was in a room, where everything within it was totally white. It was profoundly quiet. Directly in front of me was a white throne. There was a figure sitting on the throne wearing an even more brilliant shade of white. Although I could only see from the waist down, I was certain it was God.

Throughout those moments, I had remained aware of Mary's hand in mine. But that was on my left. Suddenly, I felt someone holding my right hand as well. Who would be holding my hand in heaven?

I looked towards my right but saw no one. Puzzled, I looked down. I saw a young child standing there, holding my hand and smiling up at me. Immediately I knew this was the child we had aborted. I was mesmerized. Although nothing was said, I sensed the most amazing peace and love wash over me.

Then I had the pulling sensation once again, drawing me swiftly away. The music became progressively louder until I was standing in front of the speaker, once again feeling my entire body vibrate.

Later that night, I told Mary about the vision. I let her know our child was okay and that I believed he or she had forgiven us. It was the first time we had ever spoken of our abortion since the day we left the clinic all those years before.

~

When Mary told me she was pregnant again, I

wanted to rejoice. But after three losses, though outwardly I tried to show some pleasure, inside the weight of dread descended. Would we lose this one too? After so many crushing disappointments, it became difficult to hope.

But at Mary's twenty-week ultrasound, I was amazed at the active baby on the screen. With limber arms and leg thrashing around and a strong heartbeat evident, I could finally enter into the anticipation of our child's birth.

From the first moment I held little Jeremiah in my arms, I was hopelessly in love. I wanted to protect him fiercely from harm and to someday teach him all the things he would need to know to be equipped for the world.

As he grew, my love for my son only increased. I couldn't imagine a world without Jeremiah in it. He filled our home with joy and life.

Still, there was a haunting minor key that clashed with the joyful notes. Every time I saw Jeremiah he was a reminder of the children we were missing— especially the one we aborted. My heart broke knowing our son would never meet his siblings this side of heaven.

Although I cherished every moment I had with our son, in my heart I knew the truth. I didn't deserve him.

Journey

Several years later, Mary needed to attend a funeral. It was actually the funeral for the baby of one of her students. I knew it could be rough on her and wanted to be available later if she needed to talk.

When Mary came in that evening, something about her was different. I had expected her to be a little down, but instead, it was almost as though she was more energized. Did she not attend the funeral service after all?

Yet, as she spoke about the funeral, and especially the graveside service afterwards, I became even more puzzled. Why wasn't she still upset? What was going on?

But as soon as Mary described the panic that had descended on her in that graveyard and the message from God she had heard, I began to understand. She had cried out to the Lord, and as clearly as though He were standing right beside her, He said it was time for her to grieve her aborted baby.

It had seemed as though *I* had been grieving for our child from the moment we'd driven away from that clinic. But Mary had never shown a sign of distress. Yet as we talked, I began to see she'd been hiding from the pain—trying to push it away all those years. She had successfully hidden, even from herself, but deep down there had been an aching

63

sadness.

Mary is a unique blend of being both people-focused as well as goal-oriented. Now that she knew the Lord wanted her to pursue healing from the abortion, it shouldn't have surprised me how fast she moved. That very day she had discovered a Christian-based retreat called Rachel's Vineyard.

Once I understood she wanted me to go to the retreat with her, I almost flatly refused. It was the last thing I wanted to do. But eventually, I gave in when I saw how much it meant to my wife.

~

The day we were on our way to the retreat center, whatever nerve I had in reserves was gone. Secretly, I had hoped something would happen to cause us to cancel the trip. At that point, even a natural disaster would have been preferable. I tried everything I could to change Mary's mind, including suggesting we stop in a town we were passing and have a little romantic getaway. Just the two of us.

I should have known she couldn't be deterred. She rarely was if she was truly determined. But the closer we got to our destination, the more it felt like there was a noose around my neck, cutting off my ability to take more than a shallow breath. As the miles grew shorter, the noose grew tighter.

When we arrived, Mary gave me her signature smile and squeeze of my hand that said, "Relax, everything's going to be okay." Only this time, I couldn't imagine how that could be true.

As we were walking up, I saw a man with his back to us. Good. At least I wouldn't be the only man there. But the relief was short-lived once he turned around and there was a black and white collar around his neck. Great. A man of the cloth. No way would he be able to relate to what I'd been through.

Later the next day, I surprised myself by approaching Father Malone. I had been watching him, and my gut said he was truly genuine.

Eventually, I got enough courage to ask the question burning inside me: "When is it going to stop hurting?"

He looked at me for a moment. "That depends on you. How long are you going to keep blaming yourself?"

What could I say? I couldn't imagine *not* blaming myself. The decision to abort our child may have been mutual, but I took responsibility for it. In my head, I knew God's forgiveness was available for the vilest of sins, but my heart wasn't so sure. And how would I ever be able to forgive myself?

As we talked, Father Malone's quiet strength gave

me a measure of comfort. Though I wasn't able to fully embrace God's forgiveness yet, I felt less alone.

On the last day, we wrote letters to our child. When Mary started to read hers, almost immediately she began to weep. Not just a little bit. Within minutes, it was as though a river had overflowed its banks. For a few moments, she couldn't even speak.

Watching her grief shook me to the core. In all the years I had known my wife I had never seen her shed a single tear. I'd always assumed Mary simply wasn't the type who cried. That being the only girl with so many brothers she'd learned to be tough. Crying wasn't tolerated on a football field. Now, I saw my view had been very flawed. That she had been deeply wounded by the abortion, and my heart longed to comfort hers.

The weekend became a catalyst for healing in both our lives. I wasn't comfortable talking about the abortion in the group setting. I don't think I shared much. But it helped to hear other people's stories and to know that I wasn't alone.

Most of all, what I took away from our time at Rachel's Vineyard was the gift of hope.

~

That weekend became the first of many. Mary and I went on to serve as part of a support team at

Rachel's Vineyard. I made myself available for any help needed, while Mary immediately began doing what she was born to do … listening to women's hearts and helping them find healing. Eventually, she trained to work officially as the counselor.

Father Malone and I went on to have many more conversations. He possessed a rare combination of gentleness and strength, as well as great wisdom. I will always be grateful for his friendship.

I marvel at the change in my wife. She still displays great strength, but the walls of self-protection have crumbled. Her gifts of grace and understanding have ministered to so many. God has wrought a miracle in her life: bringing beauty from ashes.

All those years, the enemy of our souls had deceived us. We believed the whispered lie that said we were alone in our suffering. That by remaining silent we were protecting the other from further wounding.

But God loved us too much to leave us in deception and pain. The day He spoke to Mary in that graveyard was her "burning bush moment." In a very real sense, it was mine as well. The Lord knew the condition of our hearts, and in His perfect timing, He revealed in order to heal. He called us out of the wilderness of our silence and suffering, and into the freedom of truth and forgiveness. I will never stop praising God for so great a love!

I look forward to the day when our whole family will finally be together. There are four children waiting for us in heaven. The Lord revealed that our aborted child was a little girl. We named her Sara Jean. The three babies we miscarried were named Susan Lavonne, B.J., and Joseph Christian. It's exciting to know that someday Jeremiah will meet his brothers and sisters.

Recently, I reflected back to the conversation I had with Father Malone that first weekend we met.

When is it going to stop hurting?

Well, that depends on you. How long are you going to keep blaming yourself?

There is no doubt that I have come a long way from where I once was. I have experienced a greater measure of healing than I ever thought possible. But since my abortion remains very painful, does that mean I'm still blaming myself? Still trying to make myself pay for a debt that has already been satisfied? Perhaps so.

Father God,

I bring this pain to You now. You never intended me to carry such an enormous burden. I sinned against my child and against You when I chose death that day. But You took on my sins in Your own body as You hung on that cross. Your blood was sufficient to wash away *my sins. <u>All</u> my sins. Help me to stop holding a grudge against myself, and to choose to forgive myself. It is not possible for me to pay such an enormous price. But I praise You, Jesus, that <u>You</u> have already paid the debt in full! Father, I choose to leave this heavy load of guilt and shame at Your feet and to fully embrace the forgiveness and freedom You died to give me.*

In Your mighty name, I pray, Jesus, amen.

"Come to me, all of you who are weary and carry heavy burdens, and I will give you rest. Take my yoke upon you. Let me teach you because I am humble and gentle at heart, and you will find rest for your souls. For my yoke is easy to bear, and the burden I give you is light."

Matthew 11:28-30 (NLT)

Ribbon Reflection

Meeting with Tom showed me more than ever that men are capable of grieving just as deeply and with as much regret as women who are post-abortive. That's not to say all men respond in this way, but there are many broken men in need of healing. I am so grateful for Tom's heart to offer hope to other men struggling with a past abortion.

In the strictest sense of the word, a man is incapable of having a physical abortion. However, the ripple effect of abortion, particularly when he has been intimately involved in the decision to end his child's life, causes deep emotional and spiritual scars. In a sense, he "earns" the right to say he's had an abortion.

This is no rite of passage, but rather an enormous weight that was clearly evident during my interview with Tom. Both the pain and deep regret was palpable, even after thirty-five years.

Where do you go when the weight that you're carrying becomes too great? Our Lord invites us to come to Him and lay our burdens down.

Let's go on a little trip to get away for a while.

You're driving along a winding road, consumed by a million things weighing you down. Around a curve, then breaking through the trees, you see a beautiful log cabin.

Drawn by the warm glow of the windows and the scent of burning wood coming from the stone chimney, you walk up the path to the front door. Before you even knock, the door swings wide.

Standing before you is Jesus. His face lit up with a huge smile; He gives you a welcoming embrace. Like a good host, He offers to take whatever you've brought with you. Did you bring your agenda? Your list of to-dos? Jesus will take them for now. Feeling lighter somehow, you look down at your cell phone and sheepishly hand it over as well, so you can enjoy an uninterrupted visit.

When Jesus gestures to what's slung over your shoulder, however, you shrink back, tightening your grip. You don't even want Jesus to see what you're holding, let alone touch it.

The bag contains everything you've ever said, thought or done, that brings you shame. It's what makes you feel disqualified to come to Him in the first place. Just when you are about to turn around and run out the door, Jesus puts His hand on your shoulder and looks into your eyes.

71

What He says takes your breath away—three words which have such power.

"It is finished."

As comprehension dawns, you cling to the words, like a lifeline for someone who's drowning. Looking into His eyes, you see the truth—Jesus already paid the debt for every sin you've ever committed, or ever will commit. So why are you still holding on to it all, unwilling to let go?

With tears streaming down your face, you hand over everything you've been carrying for far too long.

Without hesitation, Jesus throws it onto the burning logs in the fireplace. There you watch as the burdens of your sin, your shame, and regret, burst into flames. Although you anticipate a foul odor, instead, the room is quickly filled with a sweet aroma.

Suddenly, a heaviness is lifted off your shoulders. No longer carrying the weight of the world and your own sin, you can hardly believe the contrast. The two of you sit together in front of the cozy fire. Now, with nothing between, you lean into Christ's embrace—enveloped with the purest sense of love and joy imaginable. Peace washes over you, and the sense that you are forgiven … that you are finally home.

Going Deeper

1. In Tom's story, what happened to his younger sister deeply affected him. His determination to never give his father the opportunity to exert control in his life the way he saw it played out in Jill's, was a heavy factor when faced with the decision regarding an unplanned pregnancy.

    a. Looking back, can you identify circumstances in your life which influenced decisions you now wish you could reverse?

2. In a sense, part of Tom was left in that waiting room. The man who wanted to rescue both Mary and his child from the abortion felt deep shame, regret, and even self-loathing when he didn't act on that powerful desire to protect. The words "I didn't use that time right..." still echo, leaving an ache in my own heart.

    a. If you had the chance to "use that time right," what would you do differently?

3. Please share something that you so deeply regret it's as though your life remains stuck in that place.

4. Imagine you actually went on a drive and met Jesus at a cabin.

a. What are some of the barriers that might hinder your ability to connect with Him?

b. What might be included in the "bag" slung over your own shoulder?

c. What might it feel like to truly be free of the shame, guilt and self-loathing we all carry around? Is anything preventing you from laying those burdens down?

Traci's Story

Distant

Most people wrinkled their noses when they were anywhere near a pig farm, but for me, the odor was so familiar, it didn't bother me at all. I loved growing up in such a wide-open space. As far as I was concerned, the fact that my dad raised hogs, as well as crops, was a wonderful thing.

I came along much later than my two older brothers. Being the baby and the only girl had its advantages. Although I was a surprise to my parents, it wasn't an unpleasant one.

Dad was a quiet man, and for the most part kept to himself. He worked extremely hard, leaving the house before dawn and often returning to the barn after supper. He cared about his family, but he didn't really know how to connect with us. Even when he was in the same room, often it would seem as though he were somewhere else.

The time of the year I felt closest to Dad was during the harvest. I loved autumn; the crisp, cool air, the smell of burning leaves, and roasting marshmallows over a bonfire. But what I loved more than anything was getting to ride in the combine with my father.

There wasn't enough room for me to sit up front with Dad but I would create a cozy space in the flat area behind his seat. With blankets to lay on, books to read and even a few toys to play with, I was set for our adventure. We couldn't really talk because of all the noise the combine made, but we would talk a little when we stopped to eat our lunch. I just loved that my dad wanted me with him and that we could spend all that time together.

The real force in our home was my mother. No one questioned who was in charge. She had a way of carrying herself that communicated self-confidence, and she was capable of doing anything she set her mind to.

When I showed up unexpectedly, my mother was thrilled. She had always wanted a girl and delighted in playing "dress up" with me. I didn't really mind. But when I was home or playing at a friend's house, I was always in cut-off jeans and an old t-shirt.

I was a tomboy—roaming the woods, climbing trees and exploring the barn in search of new kittens or piglets. Once I was a little older, I was given a dirt bike and loved riding it all over the farm.

I know my parents loved me. I think in many ways they were proud of me. But they were part of a generation that wasn't demonstrative. I don't recall ever being hugged or hearing the words "I love you." It was more important that you showed you cared for your family through the things you did for them.

My brother, Greg, was twelve years older than me.

He had a similar temperament as my father, except he was more affectionate. Because of our age difference, he was more like a kind uncle than a brother. He still lived at home when I was a teenager but was gone so much I hardly ever saw him.

Robby was eight years older than me. If Greg was the kind brother, Robby was the mean one. Often, he was downright cruel. Like the time he took me on a motorcycle ride. I was excited until he suddenly stopped some distance from the house and made me get off the bike. He drew a circle in the dirt and made me sit inside it. I was ordered not to move a muscle, let alone to dare leave the circle for any reason until he returned or he would kill me. Was he serious? Probably not, but at eight, I totally believed him. I was terrified and didn't budge an inch for hours until Robby finally returned with Thunder.

Technically, Thunder was my pony. But riding anything with four legs was never my idea of fun, and this particular pony was quite wild and scared me to death. Robby insisted I get on Thunder and ride back to the house.

I begged Robby not to make me, but he threw me up onto Thunder's back, slapping his flank hard. Without a saddle or reins, I grabbed onto the pony's mane for dear life as he took off flying through the cornfields, sharp blades of the stalks cutting my arms and legs.

Miraculously, I arrived at my house in one piece but covered in blood from all the cuts. By that point, I had been crying hysterically and must have looked a sight. Screaming for help before I even made it to the house, I was so grateful when Dad ran out and lifted me off Thunder's back. Robby had already returned, and it was one of the few times I ever remember Dad yelling at him, although I don't recall if he got in any trouble for what he'd done.

I tried to tell Mom that I didn't like being left with Robby because he was so mean, but she always said I was exaggerating—that he was only teasing. All I know is when Mom left him in charge, I would barricade myself in my room the entire time, not even risking a trip to the bathroom.

Why was I so terrified of him? Was it because he played cruel "jokes" on me? Or was there more to it? I'm not sure. I only know I'd have felt a lot safer if he'd lived someplace else.

Together

I went on my first date when I was sixteen. John was nice enough; he just wasn't very exciting. We dated for about a year.

Scott was a whole different story. I could hardly believe it when he asked me out. He was the brother of one of my friends, and I'd had a crush on him for years. I was seventeen, and he was nineteen. Why would a good-looking high school graduate want anything to do with me?

A few years earlier his mother and one of his two brothers were involved in a car accident. Both were killed instantly. After that, Scott's father spent most of his time partying and drinking. Scott and his younger brother practically raised themselves. I think I had fallen a bit in love with him even back then—my heart hurting for him from a distance.

Scott had received a large insurance settlement as a result of the accident, so when we began dating he drove a nice car and had plenty of money. He took me out often and was always very generous.

For three years we dated off and on, becoming sexually active early in our relationship. But Scott didn't seem to understand the word "faithful," and on several occasions, I discovered he was cheating on me. I broke up with him many times, but somehow always ended up taking him back. Just

81

after my high school graduation, I started feeling sick to my stomach, especially in the morning. Then, I realized I'd missed my period. The mere thought of being pregnant was paralyzing.

I could <u>not</u> have a baby at that point in my life. I was due to start college in the fall and had no doubt I'd lose my scholarship if they knew I was pregnant. And what about my parents? They were so proud of me for earning that scholarship. What would they think of me if I were really pregnant?

I told Scott about my suspicion, and he immediately brought up abortion. That was okay with me since the last thing I wanted right then was a baby. All I knew was that I was an eighteen-year-old girl with my whole life in front of me. I didn't give other options a second thought. I didn't feel I had other options. We decided if I were pregnant we would "take care of it."

The next day, I went to Maternal Services—but there was nothing maternal about the place. I kept telling myself I couldn't possibly be pregnant. The pill was 99% effective when properly administered. I had been pretty good about taking it every day before school. I'd only missed one here or there. Surely that was good enough.

A woman took me to a back room and asked when my last period was. Then I was given a cup to take to the bathroom to provide a urine sample. It didn't take long for her to return, telling me the test was positive.

In a split second, I felt the walls closing in on me. Even though I had known there was a *possibility* of being pregnant, hearing the word "positive" made me feel as though I would be sick right then and there. This could not be happening.

The woman asked what I was going to do. When I said I didn't know, she took me to a small, closet-sized room with a phone sitting on a desk. She showed me the information about a place that performed abortions. I could call right then and make an appointment.

Just like that? So I did. My appointment was scheduled for three days later.

Later that night, I saw Scott. He said he would go with me and help me pay for an abortion. That sealed the deal. There was no talk of having the baby and keeping it or of putting it up for adoption. I was going to have an abortion and solve our problem. No one else besides us would ever have to know.

I told my mom that Scott and I were going to an amusement park for the day. It was miles away and would account for all the hours we would be gone.

The car ride to the city was awkward. I had no idea what to expect, and my mind was spinning with grim possibilities. I wish I could say Scott was supportive, but he wasn't. It's not as if he were unkind; he just seemed to be a million miles away. I needed someone to lean on, but I was on my own.

Details about the time at the abortion facility are hazy. There's no picture in my head of what the clinic looked like or the room where the abortion took place. I don't even remember if the one performing the abortion was a man or a woman. But what I do recall is seared into my memory.

I lay on the table, with just a thin sheet covering me. I felt exposed, my body trembling. My mind screamed, *Get up! Just leave!* But instead, I laid there quietly, trying to will my body to stop shaking.

Suddenly, a loud noise blasted, and I was seized with an excruciating sensation, as though all my insides were being ripped from my body. My cries were drowned out by the sound of the loud motor.

The first time I stood up after the procedure, my legs were weak, and the room started to tilt. I was told to expect some bleeding and cramping for a day or two. That was it. Before I knew it, I was with Scott, driving away from the clinic.

It all seemed so fast. It was such a blur. Was it all a horrible nightmare?

If it had been quiet on the drive to the clinic, it was

nothing compared to the thick silence that hung like a dark cloud all the way back. Huddled in my seat, the promised cramps started in with a vengeance. Closing my eyes to the bright lights of the city, I wished I could just as easily block out the sights and sounds that filled my mind.

Scott finally broke the silence by saying we would go to his brother's apartment. No one would be there, and I would be more comfortable. I was glad, thinking we would have time to talk about what had just happened. At least I wouldn't be alone.

Walking from the car to the apartment I felt as though a truck had hit me. The cramping in my abdomen had gotten much stronger, coming in waves. The room began to spin, and I lay down on the couch, curling into a ball. I wished I had the kind of mom who was comforting, who would come and hold me, telling me that somehow everything would be all right.

But my mom certainly wasn't like that, and she would never know. No one would.

Scott had been clanking around in the kitchen, when he came out, handing me a sandwich. Then, grabbing the car keys, he headed for the door. A muffled, "I'm going out for a while," is all I got before the door shut behind him.

Really? Was he just going to leave me like that? Just

go have fun while I lay there, wondering what would happen next? How did I end up here?

This wasn't how it was supposed to be.

A part of me longed to call Kathy. There was no doubt in my mind that my closest and dearest friend would drop whatever she was doing the minute she knew I needed her. That's the kind of do-or-die friendship we had.

But what was I going to say? "Hey, I just had an abortion, and now I'm falling apart?" Especially when I hadn't even bothered to tell her I was pregnant in the first place? And what would she say about what I had done? As much as I knew she loved me, I had no idea how she would react to the whole mess.

No, even while the emotions threatened to overwhelm, I made a decision. I was going to suck it up and move on. What was done was done. I just needed to shove it all down, and things would be fine.

So that's what I did. I walked away from everything. No regret, no remorse, no tears. It was like it had never happened. I went on with my life. I spent my weekends out having fun with my friends–drinking and partying, taking chances, meeting people and living life. I was going to be just fine.

Wild

Scott and I were still together, although things were rapidly falling apart. It had always been somewhat rocky between us, even when I had been enamored by his charm and good looks. The cool car and fun, carefree lifestyle had also been a big draw. Now that the veneer was definitely worn off, it was as if I were truly seeing him for the first time. I didn't much like what I saw.

A few months after the abortion, I spent a day shopping with Kathy. We were exhausted after hitting all our favorite spots. Just as I was dropping her off at her place, she asked me what was wrong.

I tried to act like I didn't know what she was talking about, but Kathy is nothing if not persistent. So in her blunt, not-so-kid-glove approach she said, "Do you think I'm blind? I don't know what's going on, but you're different. You may act like you're the life of the party with everyone else, but I *know* you. What gives?"

So I told her everything. I suppose it was inevitable. How do you keep something like that from your best friend? And even though she didn't say she agreed with what I had done, she made it clear she still loved me. That she wasn't going anywhere.

It was such a relief not to have to hold the secret inside for another moment. I was glad someone besides Scott knew about it, especially since he acted as though nothing had ever happened. Of course, Kathy was the only person I would ever admit my abortion to.

Now that I saw Scott in a new light, it wasn't flattering. He was reckless, he didn't have a job, and he had blown all the inheritance money he'd received only a couple of years before. He had even had his license suspended for a drunk driving charge.

On top of all that, he no longer treated me like I was special. He'd become increasingly dependent on me and, at the same time, more possessive and demanding. I couldn't go anywhere without an interrogation as to what I was doing or who I was with. He drank too much and was rough, although he never *really* hurt me. At least not physically.

Then I met Steve. He was a wonderful guy who treated me with respect. I hadn't even realized how much Scott put me down until I compared that behavior with how Steve treated me. He wanted to know everything about me and made me feel as though I could do anything I wanted to do. He made me want to dream again.

Seeing the contrast between the two men made it easy for me to finally walk away from such a toxic relationship. I put an end to that chapter of my life and began to see Steve on a regular basis.

A couple of months later, I was at a bar with a friend when Scott walked in. Immediately, he began trying to get me to dance with him, but I flatly refused his advances. I couldn't believe he actually still thought there was a chance that he could get me back.

When I was leaving the bar, Scott followed me out to the parking lot. He was obviously quite intoxicated, and things became ugly. Before I knew what was happening, he'd hit me in the face, knocking me to the pavement.

For a moment, I lay there dazed, holding my cheek. What had just happened? I managed to get in my car and took off, while Beth, the friend I was with, chose to stay behind.

A few weeks later, I was at Kathy's place when I noticed a letter lying on her coffee table. Seeing my name, curiosity got the best of me. The letter was from Beth, and it was about the night Scott hit me. She wrote that she had gone back into the bar with Scott, and he'd told her about my abortion. According to her, Scott claimed he wasn't even sure if the child had been his. Beth also expressed how appalled and horrified she was at what I had done.

How *dare* Scott tell anyone my business? And to insinuate that I was sleeping around with other guys besides? My hands tightly closed into fists while my head instantly began to throb. I had a strong desire to punch something. Or some*one*. At that moment, if I'd been anywhere near Scott, I don't think his pretty face would've been quite so pretty anymore.

And what about Beth? I had never really been crazy about her anyway, so dropping that friendship would be easy. Obviously, I wasn't concerned that Beth told Kathy about the abortion. She already knew. But who else was she going to tell?

Yet what could I do about it? In the end, I decided just to let it go. I hadn't seen Scott since that night at the bar, and the last thing I wanted to do was to stir up that hornet's nest. I was dating Steve and going to college. I had moved on.

Then, out of the blue, Scott showed up at my apartment. He said he was on his way to Missouri where he'd just gotten a great job. He couldn't leave town without asking me to go with him.

I'm sure my mouth must have dropped wide open. What? Just drop everything and run away with him? For a moment, I was speechless. After everything, the man had the audacity to believe he still had a chance with me.

As he walked away, I almost felt sorry for him.

Silence

A couple of years later, Steve and I were married. I loved him with all my heart. Before long we had two little boys and a life anyone would envy. But something wasn't right.

Although Steve knew everything else about my life, I had never revealed my past abortion. I just hadn't been able to even say the word.

I could usually manage to avoid thinking about the abortion unless the subject came up. Then I would panic. What should I say if someone asked my opinion? What if someone guessed my secret? The very thought of being discovered gave me chills and made my heart pound like a drum gone crazy.

Hearing the word "abortion" was like hearing my name shouted across the room.

Going to the doctor was stressful, too. I never admitted to any other pregnancies besides my living children, but I was so afraid that somehow they would discover my secret.

Needing a change of scenery one day, I packed up my boys for a road trip to "Aunt" Kathy's. She'd married and started a whole new life in a different state, but we still called each other often to stay in touch.

Our children played together well while we reminisced about our high school days. After the kids had been settled in for the night, Kathy grew more serious. She told me she'd given her life to Jesus. That it was as though a huge burden had lifted off her shoulders.

It was like she was speaking a different language. *Gave her life to Jesus?* What did that even mean? I had gone to church at times growing up. So had she. Sure, it wasn't that often, but it was enough to get by.

This sounded radical. Maybe even a little crazy. She said we were all sinners in need of a Savior. That Jesus Christ had come from heaven deliberately to die a cruel death.

I knew that Jesus had died on a cross, but Kathy said Jesus had come to earth on *purpose*. That He had allowed Himself to be crucified in order to save us from our sins and to offer us a whole new life.

Until that moment, I had never heard that Jesus died *for me* … that He had taken my place. I wasn't sure what to do with that information.

The next day, Kathy was pretty straight forward. She told me I had a choice to make. If I chose to put my trust in Jesus, He would forgive me of all my sins and make me a brand-new creation.

Then she asked if the abortion bothered me. It was the first time we had spoken of it since the day I'd told her years before. I knew she wasn't bringing the subject up to judge me. She simply knew me well enough to understand the abortion was probably one of the sins in my life that bothered me the most. She quoted a verse from the Bible, "Though your sins be as scarlet they shall be as white as snow."

What would that be like? To actually feel clean? To not have to carry the stain of my abortion anymore? I was sure it was too good to be true. Nevertheless, it stirred a longing in my soul.

Back home, I couldn't stop thinking about everything Kathy had shared. My thoughts were like dark clouds gathering as my abortion filled my mind like a mighty storm. I was overwhelmed with a sense of guilt and shame. After pushing the experience away for so long, I could no longer escape the truth.

I desperately wanted to be rid of such a heavy burden. So, finally, I cried out to God, begging Him to forgive my sins. Especially for taking my own child's life. I invited Him to come into my heart and to change me.

For the first time, I wept over my abortion. It was as if something inside me broke loose, and a flood of tears came pouring out. Sitting there in my bedroom, I was filled with a certainty that my baby had been a girl. Was the Lord speaking to me? I wasn't sure, but I decided to name her "Nicole Renee."

Kathy had told me about a verse in the book of Matthew. I found my Bible and wiping the dust off, looked up Matthew 11:28. It said:

> *"Come to Me, all you who are weary and burdened, and I will give you rest. Take My yoke upon you and learn from Me, for I am gentle, and humble in heart, and you will find rest for your souls. For My yoke is easy and My burden is light." (ESV)*

As I sat before the Lord, I felt my burdens lift. After years of guilt, there was a lightness in my heart. I was *forgiven*.

I immediately went to tell Steve what I had just experienced. I also told him about my abortion. It felt good to finally have the courage to be completely honest with him.

He was compassionate about the abortion, and he even tried to be excited for me about my new relationship with God. He told me if I ever needed to talk about the abortion again, he would be there for me. I was so grateful to have such a wonderful and loving husband.

After that, I called Kathy more often, peppering her

with questions. She was thrilled about my decision. I realized even though I had attended church off and on when I was growing up, I knew almost nothing about the Bible. Was I distracted and simply missed the teaching? Even the account of David and Goliath was new to me. On Kathy's suggestion, I purchased a children's Bible and read it aloud to my kids. That way we were all learning at the same time.

I still struggled in many ways, especially because of my abortion. Thankfully, after receiving Christ's forgiveness, I no longer looked at abortion as something unforgivable.

But how did I forgive myself?

~

Many years and two babies later, I was taken aback when I saw I had a Facebook message from Scott. After so much time, what could he possibly want? There wasn't a personal message. Besides his name, all that was there was a song called "Red Rag Top," by Tim McGraw.

When I read the words, later listening to the song, it nearly took my breath away. If I hadn't known better, I would have thought the lyrics were written for us. Right down to my green eyes.

What an achingly sad song, about a young couple who find themselves expecting a child and choose abortion as their way out. The lyrics made it clear that the abortion still bothered the man, all those years later.

Did that mean the abortion bothered Scott? I had assumed since he'd never brought the subject up again, it had meant what we had done didn't matter to him.

Now, looking at the lyrics, I was no longer so sure. "Well you do what you do, and you pay for your sins, and there's no such thing as what might have been, that's a waste of time, drive you out of your mind..." (Quote from Red Rag Top, by Tim Mc Graw)

If the song reflected how Scott felt after all those years, then the "aftershocks" from our decision that day were still causing tremors in both our lives.

The tears began to flow, triggered by the haunting lyrics.

Scott wasn't the only one in need of more healing.

Revealed

After a few years, I was thrilled when Steve made a decision to follow Christ. Later, we would both make an even deeper commitment to surrender our lives completely to the Lord.

One weekend, Steve planned a spiritual retreat for the two of us. It was an opportunity to focus on each other and on our relationship with God. During that weekend we decided to write a letter to God, confessing times in our lives when we had deliberately sinned against Him. It was a private moment between ourselves and God, then together, we each took our letters and threw them into a small bonfire. Watching the papers ignite and burn was a beautiful picture of how God removes our sins from us as far as the east is from the west.

The next morning, I reflected on that experience, writing in my journal a verse I was drawn to:

"Create in me a clean heart, Oh God, and renew a right spirit within me." Psalm 51:10 (ESV)

Later, during a few quiet moments, I clearly heard in my spirit, *You need to write out your abortion story.*

It took me by surprise, to say the least, but I knew it was the Lord and that I needed to listen to His voice. So I rearranged my schedule and sat down right away. The words seemed to pour from my pen.

That night, we met with our small group. On the video series we'd been watching, the leader suggested we share something deeply personal that no one else in the group knew about. He even used the example of a past abortion. Instantly my mouth went dry, and my palms became slick.

So, this was why God had told me that very day to write out my story. It was the next step in the healing process—a step I did not want to take. But, I wanted to be obedient to the Lord, knowing He always had my best in mind.

So with shaking hands and a deep, steadying breath, I told my discussion group I'd had an abortion. I was scared to death, but they were all so loving and tender. I didn't sense a critical spirit in anyone. I had been hiding for so long, but God was showing me there was freedom in the light.

The next day I woke up refreshed. Spending quiet moments with God, I poured out my gratitude for His goodness towards me. I had not wanted to step through that door by telling others about my abortion, but the Lord had definitely used it for good.

A few minutes later, Steve came in. Immediately, I could tell something was wrong. He told me we needed to talk. Normally I liked surprises, but judging by his expression I knew this wasn't the kind of surprise I was going to enjoy.

He told me there was something he had not included on his sheet the day before; something he needed to tell me about.

I tried to dissuade him. That whatever it was not to worry about it. I wanted so badly to stop the words from coming out of his mouth. But I couldn't.

"Babe, I'm so sorry. I know you don't want to hear this. I never wanted to hurt you, and I wish with all my heart it wasn't true. But, the words are burning in my soul, and they have to come out."

He took a deep breath, "I had an affair."

At first, it was as if everything froze. All I could see and hear were those four words, blooming into a billboard sign in my mind. "I HAD AN AFFAIR." Steve kept talking, but I couldn't hear anything else.

Later, he would have to repeat the details of his betrayal, because nothing was getting past those words ricocheting in my brain. I stood there, hands clenched at my sides. I wanted to scream, *No! Why did you go and ruin everything? It was bad enough that you did it, but why did you have to tell me? Couldn't you have just dealt with it between you and God?*

Had I had an inkling of his infidelity somewhere buried deep inside? Did I believe not hearing about it could somehow protect my heart?

I don't know how I responded to Steve that day. I

just shut down. I needed time on my own to process what I'd just been told.

By the next morning, my whole world seemed dark. I was plunged into a whirlwind of ever-changing emotions, one minute wanting to break something, the next wondering if there could be any tears left. I found it hard to get out of bed. Sometimes I didn't see the point.

Walking around in a fog, I tried to make sense of the senseless. How could he have done what we had promised each other we would never do? How could I ever trust him again? What had this woman had that I was missing? Why hadn't I been enough?

Feelings and thoughts collided into a chaotic mess, and gradually I was inching my way toward the edge of a cliff. I was barely hanging on.

Even though the affair had happened years earlier, before Steve had surrendered his life to God, that didn't make it any less painful. All I wanted was to have my life back, to the way things used to be. But that wasn't possible.

And where was God in all of this? Why had He allowed it to happen? Why did it have to come out right *then*, on that particular day? Hadn't I had enough to deal with? Hadn't I just been obedient to His leading me to write about my abortion, then to willingly share such a deeply personal thing with a group of people? Just when I thought I was on the path to further healing, I was knocked back down again.

Steve and I struggled for quite some time after his confession. Just when it seemed we were making progress toward healing our marriage, something would happen to rip the scab off, revealing the gaping wound beneath.

But if I had learned anything on my journey with the Lord, it was this: God was God, and I was not. While I saw things through a proverbial hole in the fence, my Heavenly Father had a supernatural view. He saw every conceivable angle, including the past, present and future. He knew how everything would turn out. How he would use it together for good. I did not.

Gradually, I realized I had to let go. To surrender it all to Him. I had to face my own sinfulness and be willing to extend forgiveness to my husband.

I wish I could say the process only took a few months. The truth is it was over a year before I sensed the darkness begin to lift.

~

About a year later, I received a last-minute invitation from a dear friend. She wanted me to attend a volunteer training at a local pregnancy center. On a whim, I agreed. I surprised myself by deciding to volunteer. One of the requirements for volunteers who'd had a past abortion was to participate in their post-abortion healing study, *Forgiven and Set Free*. Reluctantly I agreed.

The whole experience was nothing like I thought it would be. The leaders were warm and accepting, and the two other women seeking healing became so much more than friends.

When the study was nearly over, we were encouraged to ask the Lord what we could do to release our child back to Him. One of us wrote a letter. Another wrote a poem. I painted a picture.

I'd always enjoyed painting but hadn't done so in quite a while. That day, when I sat before my easel, everything just flowed. Peaks and valleys in the background, five long-stemmed flowers in the foreground, each representing one of my precious children. The centers of the flowers were colored according to each child's birthstone. I chose a beautiful lavender shade for the center of Nicole Renee's, acknowledging that if I had not aborted her, she would have been born in the month of February. I also printed out Psalm 139:13-16 (ESV), and placed it on the back of the painting:

...You formed my inward parts; You knitted me together in my mother's womb. I praise You, for I am fearfully and wonderfully made. Wonderful are Your

works; my soul knows it very well. My frame was not hidden from You, when I was being made in secret, intricately woven in the depths of the earth. Your eyes saw my unformed substance; in Your book were written, every one of them, the days that were formed for me, when as yet there were none of them.

As the three of us approached the table that night, although we each took our own turn, it felt like we were doing it *together*. We had been around that table all those evenings, as one by one we peeled back the painful layers of our lives, exposing them to the light of God's love and forgiveness. It forged a bond between us that has not diminished over time.

In addition to those precious friendships, the greatest gift I received through that experience was the ability to forgive myself. I believed in God's forgiveness long before I was willing to forgive the one on my list that I harbored the greatest bitterness towards … myself.

I will always regret my abortion, but I will no longer condemn myself. Instead, I will choose to walk in the freedom and forgiveness that Jesus purchased for me.

I am grateful to say that today, my marriage is stronger than it's ever been. God continues to redeem that time I once thought was lost forever.

Looking at God's "ribbon of redemption" in my life gives me courage. I now know that no matter what happens in this life, I can trust God to use it all together for good.

"I sought the LORD and He answered me and delivered me from all my fears. Those who look to Him are radiant, and their faces shall never be ashamed."

Psalm 34:4-5 (ESV)

Ribbon Reflection

I experienced many blessings during the process of writing *Ribbon of Redemption*. One of the most delightful of those blessings was meeting at length with each of the people who shared their stories. Those were precious moments as we met heart to heart, in a place so tender, I had the sense that I was on holy ground. It was such an honor to be invited into that sacred space.

Traci was the first person who agreed to share her story. Although she remains anonymous, her generosity and vulnerability is no small thing. I am eternally grateful for these seven brave souls and pray abundant blessings over them and over all those they love!

One of the things I noticed in Traci's story was how her abortion not only impacted her but several others as well. The one that surprised her the most was Scott, the father of her aborted baby. Although he appeared to be unfazed by the abortion, if the song he sent her was any indication, he was still dealing with the "aftershocks" of that decision many years later.

James Kounin was the first to coin the phrase "ripple effect." What happens when you drop a small stone on the surface of a pond? It creates ripples. Concentric circles splaying out from where the stone plunged, in an ever widening diameter. The rings may look pretty, even soothing, on the surface of the water. But what about when you apply the same principle to the decision to end a life?

The Merriam-Webster Dictionary defines ripple effect as "A spreading, pervasive, and usually unintentional effect or influence."

People seeking to influence a woman to abort, make it sound as though it is a simple, individualistic choice. No one points out how "pervasive" that choice will become. It is only after the woman (and those who were involved in the decision making process) is on the other side of abortion that she begins to experience the magnitude of that single decision.

Almost everyone I've spoken to who has experienced an abortion admits to having been effected in very significant ways. One of those ways is how it has affected their relationships with those they love: parents, siblings, partners, spouses, children, future children, friends, coworkers ... the list is endless.

The truth is, no one is "just" an individual—we are all part of a whole, each impacting the other in ways beyond our comprehension.

All of us have made choices which resulted in consequences we now regret. But there is *hope*. With

God, it is *never too late* to begin *reversing* those "ripples." The best gift you can give yourself, and those you love, is to pursue God. Give Him the tangled strands of your life—the good, the bad, and the ugly. He can take those strands, once woven in ugliness and *re-weave* them into something truly beautiful.

Why not begin today?

Going Deeper

1. Prior to Traci's healing, she said hearing the word "abortion" spoken aloud was like hearing her name shouted across a room. Shame had become so deeply imbedded in the fabric of her being; she wore the name abortion as though it were her identity.
    a. In what ways have you allowed words or actions to identify you?
    b. If you have received Jesus as your Savior, you are a child of God. What other names does the Lord call you that might replace the labels you have attached to yourself?

2. Traci kept her abortion hidden until years later the Lord began nudging her to begin dealing with it.
    a. What does that say about God's patience?
    b. If you are post-abortive, can you think of someone you sense is trustworthy, with whom you could share your abortion story?

Layla's Story

Pain

I don't ever recall sitting down to a family meal and hearing "How was your day, honey?" Or laughing with my parents about something silly that happened to one of us. That would have been totally out of place, and cause to be on guard.

If I had to come up with a single word to describe my home life, it would be *tension*. Everyone tiptoeing around as though walking on eggshells, doing whatever it took to avoid setting my mother off. That was the very last thing we wanted to do.

Sometimes, I wondered what my parents ever saw in each other. I never saw any display of affection—only a constant friction between them. When they met, Mom already had my two brothers from a prior marriage. Did my mother just want a father for her children? Or was it the comfortable lifestyle that she craved?

When I was young, my father loved to bring me gifts. It made me feel like a beautiful princess. But Mom hated that he brought me things and paid attention to me. Often, she would insist he return the present, saying it was somehow inappropriate, or that I had misbehaved and didn't deserve it.

Still, I quickly learned if I wanted a "yes" to something, I better ask Dad. But those small victories often came at a cost. Mom would come and whisper in my ear, *Wait till your father goes to work.* Those words would send chills down my spine.

Mom wasn't always mean. In her own way, I know she loved my brothers and me. But something inside her must have been shattered long ago. Things could seem fairly peaceful one moment, and then the "good mom/bad mom" switch would be flipped. Almost as though she became a different person.

Kids from school thought I was lucky. Both my parents had successful careers, and we lived in a beautiful home. But all they saw was the facade. They had no idea how much *I* envied *them*—the ones with parents who loved each other. Parents who seemed to enjoy spending time with their children. Inside I felt like an orphan left out in the cold. As though my face was pressed against a windowpane, longing to be part of a loving family.

Spending time with my brothers helped so much. Whenever they were left in charge of me, I felt free to laugh and play. To just be myself. Even though Adam was ten years older than me, and Jaimie was seven years older, the three of us were very close. In many ways, they made up for what I lacked from my mother.

Adam was especially kind. He was my fierce protector. But no matter how much my brothers wanted to shield me from violent outbursts, it wasn't always possible. We weren't beaten every day, but at any given moment Mom could become enraged. The unpredictability kept me continually off balance.

~

111

The day Adam left for the Air Force was one of the saddest days of my life. Even his love for me couldn't keep him from escaping our home as soon as possible. I clung to him so tightly. I wanted to scream, *No, Adam! Please don't leave me alone with Mom! I need you!* But I didn't want him to feel bad.

My brother Jaimie had pretty much already left. At fifteen he'd joined a gang and had been in and out of juvenile hall. With both of my brothers gone my world grew even darker, as the full brunt of Mother's anger fell on me. At the age of eight, I lived in constant fear of what would happen when Mom and I were alone.

The only place I could escape the fear and anxiety was at ballet class. I had been taking ballet for years. I was surprised Mom allowed me that outlet, but I think in her own way she was proud of how well I did. Whenever I danced, it took me to a place where no one could touch me. Even when I was only warming up, the moment I began the rhythmic motions the heaviness would begin to lift. As I flowed with the music, I felt free.

Performing on a stage took that sense of freedom to a whole new level. Dancing before a captivated audience was intoxicating, and for a while, I was someone else. Someone without all the problems I faced on a daily basis.

~

With Adam gone, I felt more alone than ever before. I tried hard not to give Mom a reason to be angry, and in the very beginning, things weren't so bad. But then my parents started fighting a lot more. Before long, mornings were the worst part of the day.

My dad left for work quite early. Once the door clicked shut, against my will, my body would begin to shake. Sometimes nothing happened, and later I would find that I had drifted back to sleep.

At other times, Mom and Dad's voices would be raised, and then the front door would slam shut. Soon there would be footfalls outside my bedroom and Mom would fling open my door, reaching in to flip on the light.

Bad days began with screaming. *You lazy little brat! How dare you lay there in bed! I'm sure you heard every word between your dad and me. You're the reason our marriage is falling apart! "Daddy's little princess!"*

I tried to shield myself. Mom would grab me by my hair and drag me off the bed. Sometimes she would put her hands around my throat, squeezing until I grew lightheaded, nearly blacking out. Or she would take my pillow, pressing it down hard over my face. That was the worst—everything going completely dark; the breath trapped in my lungs. Was I going to die? Then suddenly she would just let go, leaving me gasping for air. Once she left me alone, I would give myself a minute and then start getting ready for school.

Riding the bus was one of the highlights of my day because I got to be with my best friend, Molly. I loved her like a sister, and she loved me. We were truly kindred spirits. One of the reasons we were so close was because our mothers were very much alike. Her mother didn't beat her like mine did, but she could be cruel in other ways. Molly understood that no matter how someone might appear to others, it was often not who they really were.

We always tried to find a seat in the back. On our own, we would sit huddled close, whispering in each other's ears. Our friendship helped sustain me through many difficult times.

Even though I may have just been screamed at or had my hair yanked so hard it made my scalp bleed, somehow I managed to put those memories away the moment I walked through the doors of my school. It was a place where I could be normal.

Trapped

When I turned thirteen, it seemed like I developed curves overnight, and my emotions were all over the map. Dad started acting really awkward around me. He hardly ever spoke to me unless it was really necessary. He began coming home late in addition to leaving so early. At a time when I needed my father the most, he decided to check out.

I'd always wanted to tell Dad what really happened to me whenever he wasn't around. Rehearsing it in my head, I had imagined how shocked he would be. How he would swoop in and save me.

But I was also afraid. What if Mom was right? What if I told Dad and he didn't even believe me? Where would I be then?

It seemed as if everyone I ever loved ended up leaving, one way or another.

~

It was the summer before my freshman year of high school. Mom had been calmer lately, and I began to hope things might get better.

One day I came home after hanging out with my friend, Francine. Even though Mom should have still been at work, she was already there. The minute she saw me, she flew into a rage. "Where have you been? Here I thought you'd done all your chores, and I find a complete mess!"

Reaching behind my head, she yanked me by my ponytail, knocking me off-balance as I fell to the tile floor. My knee hit the hard surface and a shockwave radiated up my leg. Crying out, I scrambled to my feet, trying to get away. I was bracing for the next assault when there was a knock on the front door. For a moment, I thought Mom would ignore it, but after the second set of knocks she glared at me, then headed towards the front door in the living room.

As soon as she walked out, I grabbed my coat and purse, running out the back door. My head throbbed where she'd pulled my hair, and my knee ached, but I quickly ran up to the corner gas station and used the pay phone to call Francine. Soon she and her mom were picking me up.

I knew, this time, I needed to break the silence. I was tired of trying to protect myself. When I told Francine's mom about the abuse she was appalled. She didn't even want to let me go back home, but somehow I convinced her that I would be okay. She gave me the phone number for Social Services if things ever went too far again.

Walking back home, I decided I was done playing the cat and mouse game with my mother. Stepping in the front door I found Mom. Looking her straight in the eye, I told her if she ever laid her hand on me again I was reporting her. I also told her I was telling my father everything.

Something in my expression must have let her know I was serious because she didn't start screaming or hitting me. I could hardly believe it. Was that all I had needed to do? Just stand up to her instead of cowering in the corner?

Later that night, when Dad came home, I asked if I could talk to him in private. He raised his eyebrows at the request but at least he went with me to the den. Sitting on the couch, I told him everything.

It was such a relief to finally tell him the truth. For years I had lied about so many things. The busted lips, the red marks and bruises over the years. I'd covered for my mother out of fear—what would she have done to me if I'd told?

But before I was even done the expression on his face told me everything I needed to know. He didn't believe me.

Had Mom already talked to him and warned him I would say those things? She had a way of twisting things around. Of saying I was just very rebellious and out of control; that he needed to take a bigger role in my discipline.

I had longed for the day when my father would finally understand all I had endured. When he would wrap me in his arms and tell me he was sorry—that he would give anything to take the pain away. Instead, he'd listened to my mother weave her lies.

How could he take my mother's word over mine? Hadn't he seen her fly into rages for years? Even physically attack him on several occasions? Why wouldn't he believe me?

In a moment, all my hopes had come crashing down. Unlike Cinderella, I had no fairy godmother. No handsome prince who would rescue me. No, happily ever after.

I just needed to face facts. My life was no fairytale, and I would never be anyone's princess.

~

For a while, things seemed to be better. Even though Dad didn't believe me, Mom and I were in a truce of sorts. But sometimes I caught her looking at me in a calculated way, and I knew it was just a matter of time.

One morning, I woke up to the sound of Dad cursing loudly, then a door slamming. Almost instantaneously, Mom burst into my room. Flipping on the lights, she was looming over me in seconds, grabbing me by my hair and dragging me off the bed. Fire exploded over the surface of my head, even as she screamed at me that it was *my* fault her marriage was falling apart.

All my life I had never fought back. I knew it would only make matters worse. But at that moment, in my mind's eye, I could see Adam as he had defended me time and time again. He even threatened Mom with a knife, on one occasion, in order to make her let me go.

So gathering all my courage and strength I pushed her as hard as I could, knocking her to the ground. Snatching a loose hoodie on my way out of my room to throw over my pajamas, I ran out the back door to Molly's house. She only lived a few blocks away, and at such an early hour I knew she'd be home.

This time, instead of worrying that Mom would catch me, my blood felt like it was going to pop out of my veins. Enough! I was sick of my mother ruining my life.

When Molly's mom answered the door, I told her what was going on. Thankfully she let me stay with them for several days. Since it was summer, I didn't have to worry about school and Mom didn't even seem to look for me. I just needed time to figure out what I should do. I couldn't take it any longer. This *had* to stop.

Finally, after talking to Molly and her mom I decided to report the abuse to Social Services. With Molly sitting beside me for moral support I picked up the thousand-pound receiver.

When I finally got through to the right person, I was told that I had been reported missing and therefore was considered a runaway. As such, I needed to go to the police station to turn myself in and could tell my story to them.

So Mom had covered her bases. The next thing I knew I was down at the police station being questioned by a couple of officers. They talked to me alone first and then with my parents, who had also been called to the station.

I never thought I would have to sit in the same room with my parents, or that I would be forced to listen to my Mom spinning her story. Watching the faces of the officers as Mom talked I started to lose confidence. She was so good at looking and sounding innocent. She played the role of a loving-parent-who-was-overwhelmed-by-her-out-of-control-teenaged-daughter very well.

Before I knew it, I was in my Dad's car being driven away, labeled a rebellious teenager who had run away simply because I didn't want to follow my parent's rules.

What was the use of even trying? The ones who were supposed to protect me didn't do a thing. They basically called me a liar. With my parents' upstanding reputation in the community combined with the fact that they knew a couple of police officers on the force, why did it surprise me that I was sent right back to my nightmare?

That night I told Mom if she ever touched me again I would kill her. I didn't yell, but I didn't blink either. If no one would defend me, then I would defend myself in whatever way I had to.

Mom tried to act like she didn't care what I said, but I knew I was serious. Apparently, she did too because she seemed to back down. I was safe—at least for now.

But even if the physical abuse stopped, how long would I be able to put up with the verbal attacks?

Forced

In the fall of my freshman year, I'd begun to relax a little. Although Mom hadn't suddenly become the model parent, at least I wasn't constantly looking over my shoulder. I was determined to begin to enjoy my life.

I had always had a poor self-image, but gradually I was becoming more confident. I also started disregarding my parent's rules. Whatever respect I'd had for either of them was long gone.

That's when I met Luis. As far as I was concerned, Luis was the best thing that ever happened to me. We were in a class together, and from the first day, we couldn't keep our eyes off each other. His were a gorgeous brown. They crinkled up at the corners frequently, as if they were laughing. His smile was infectious and had a way of warming my heart. How could I be sad when I was around him? More importantly, Luis was affectionate and caring. He gave me all the things I had been craving: hugs, kisses, laughter, and a sense of belonging.

Luis was sixteen and had his own car. Soon I began sneaking around with him whenever I could, reveling in the forbidden freedom. It was high time I had a little fun.

Mom no longer kept tabs on me to the degree she once had. I would lie about where I was and take off with Luis with zero remorse. Although no one believed me about the abuse the first time, she must have realized repeated accusations might actually stick to her perfect little record. She was pretty much letting me do what I wanted—within reason.

Eventually, I began fantasizing about life with Luis, far away from my parents. We would run away together, and build a home where there would only be love and understanding. Part of the picture included a baby. Someone on which to pour out all the love I had never received growing up.

At first, when I discovered I was pregnant at fifteen, I was happy. It was what I had wanted. I would raise my baby to know how special he or she was. Somehow, I would finally escape the home that still represented a prison cell. Although I wasn't being beaten, it was still such a negative atmosphere.

Initially, I kept the pregnancy a secret. It wouldn't do to have my parents or anyone else find out too soon. Except for Luis, no one else knew. He was excited about the baby, and everything seemed to be going according to plan.

But after a couple of days I couldn't help telling Molly, and somehow Molly's mom overheard us talking. That didn't seem all bad. Having an adult on my side might even be a good thing. I knew I would need help once my parents suspected I was pregnant.

Then it all backfired. Molly's mom was afraid the pregnancy was too big of a secret to keep from my mom and dad. Going straight to my parents, she told them everything, easing her conscience by asking them to be gentle. I felt as though I had just been kicked in the stomach. How could she have betrayed me like that?

My father went ballistic. Ranting and raving, he screamed that I had to get an abortion. I was appalled—how could I abort the baby I'd longed for? That I already loved?

I had never seen my father the way he was during that time. It was as if someone kidnapped my mild-mannered parent and replaced him with someone aggressive and mean. He shouted vile words at me, pointing his finger in accusation over and over. It wasn't as though I'd never heard him yell or say ugly things before, but prior to that day it had only been directed at my mother. Now, the father who had once called me his little princess relentlessly beat me down.

At first, my mother supported my decision not to abort. Even when my father threatened to divorce her and abandon us, she said, "If your dad divorces us we'll do this together."

It wasn't surprising Mom didn't side with my father—mother had always raised me to believe abortion was wrong. Soon, however, Mother stopped saying things would work out. Although she didn't actually tell me to abort, it was clear she agreed with my father.

Where would I go if they threw me out? My father never let up day in and day out. I was in a torture chamber, only the prison cell was my home, and the enemy soldier was my own father.

Finally, I lacked the energy to fight back. By the end of the week, I walked into the local Planned Parenthood. I remember the floor was black and white checkered squares. I had to look away because it made the room spin.

There were lots of other women seated in the lobby. *Are they all here for the same thing I am?* The thought made me start to cry. My mom quickly jumped up and told the receptionist they needed to take me back right away. Before I knew it, I was being whisked to the back. Had she given them more money?

The woman who took me didn't seem very professional. Her uniform was ripped and had a couple of missing buttons. She said very little, and even when she did talk she was looking somewhere over my shoulder.

Saying we needed to see how far along I was, she soon had me lying on the table with a probe on my belly. The ultrasound screen was right in front of me, in plain view. *What, they let you watch?* As soon as I saw the little baby with the strong heartbeat, I was done. I started shaking violently, hot tears coursing down my face. Inside I was screaming. *I can't do this! I don't want to do this!*

Then, as if for the first time, the woman seemed to actually see me. She looked directly at me and asked if I wanted to have an abortion. When I told her no, without another word, she let me get dressed and took me back to the lobby.

I was still shaking and crying. My parents looked startled to see me back so soon until the woman told them I "wasn't ready yet."

Dad was furious. All the way home I was berated and ridiculed, while my mom, for once, sat passively by. If the pressure had been high that first week, the intensity doubled. The worst was when my father threatened to commit suicide if I didn't go through with the abortion. He said he would not live with the shame of a fifteen-year-old daughter having a baby.

What should I do? I wasn't sure if my father was really serious, but he'd been so different during the past couple of weeks. His threat seemed quite real. I felt as though I were being torn in two.

I was being asked to make a horrific choice: the death of my child, or the death of my father.

Then, one morning Mom came into my room and begged me to abort. She said if I didn't end the pregnancy Dad would divorce her, and she'd lose everything she had worked so hard for—the beautiful house, everything they'd accumulated over the years, along with the lifestyle she was accustomed to. She said she'd made me an appointment at a different clinic where she'd been assured they would be more understanding with me and would also provide counseling.

I couldn't take it anymore. How could I possibly have this baby on my own with no support? Where would I go? It was as though I had been trying with all my might to keep the dam from breaking, but the water breached the wall, and everything broke apart.

This time, they took me to a clinic in the city. I met with a counselor who told me that it wasn't a baby at all. That it was more like a little alien. She said that it was okay—that this was what girls in my situation did.

That was the extent of my "counseling." I tried to believe what she was telling me was true. By that point, I was completely numb. My body might be present, but the rest of me was somewhere deep inside.

The abortion was quick but excruciating. I wasn't given any sedative or anesthesia. The nurse held my hand, but the doctor never looked at me or spoke one word. Worst of all was the horrifying sound of the contents of my uterus being sucked through the tube.

That would haunt me for a very long time.

~

I never told Luis about the abortion. Instead, I lied, saying I'd had a miscarriage. I didn't have the heart to tell him the truth because he had been so excited about the baby. And lies came far too easily.

For a long time, I was alone in a sea of grief and pain. Everything shut down, and all I seemed to be able to do was cry. The one thing that brought me comfort was when I drew a picture of my baby. I hadn't been able to forget the tiny image of my child on that ultrasound screen, nor did I want to. Making a tangible memory seemed to give my child value—a way of acknowledging that he or she had really existed. I also wrote a poem.

Often, I would pull the picture out of its hiding place to look at it. One day, when I reached for the page, it wasn't there. Frantically I searched my room, only to discover that the poem was missing too. Had I been careless? Did I leave them out?

I cried myself to sleep and later went into the kitchen for a drink. My mother was fixing dinner and looked up as I entered the room. When she smiled at me, I knew. It was there in her eyes; she took them.

She didn't acknowledge what she had done, and I knew it would be pointless even to ask about it. She would only lie, and I didn't want to discuss anything with her, let alone my baby.

But in those moments a darkness entered my soul. Something about her smile collided with the horror of what she and my father had forced me to do. Taking my only memory of my baby felt as if that life had been ripped from me all over again.

Only a fragment of the poem remains:
Mommy is so sorry she wasn't able to give you a chance at life.

Rebellious

I decided it was time to make a fresh start, and I focused on improving my grades. I also began hanging out with my friends again, especially Luis.

When I turned sixteen, I talked Dad into buying me a car. My father and I certainly did not have the best relationship, but he was always good at giving me presents—and now he no longer cared what Mom thought about it.

With the money I earned from my new job at the local grocery store and having my own transportation, I experienced a freedom I'd never had before. I used that freedom to sneak around with Luis whenever I could.

Then I began noticing a guy at work. Not in a romantic way—there was just something different about him. He wasn't only nice; he was *real*. His name was Jeremy, and he was passionate about God. His whole face would light up as he talked about the goodness of God, and how everyone needed Him. He spoke about Jesus as though He were right there with us, instead of being off somewhere in space. When there was a lull in customers, I loved to listen to him talk about his faith.

Jeremy invited me to youth group, and it was wonderful. The people were excited about their relationship with God and seemed so full of joy. I started to go whenever I could, and even made a few friends.

I still saw Luis though. After my parents had forced me to abort, I wasn't about to lose him too.

On one of the rare occasions my dad was home, Mom started yelling, accusing me of running around with Luis. I had gotten quite an attitude, and I told her I would see Luis anytime I wanted to. The next thing I knew, my mother had knocked me down onto the cold kitchen floor, pressing her arm across my throat. Wildly I looked over to where Dad stood, my eyes begging him to look at me and come to my rescue. Instead, he turned around and walked out of the room.

His response hit me like a cold wave, knocking me flat. Even as I fought for breath, my heart fisted inside my chest. Was it possible he hadn't seen what my mother was doing to me? What other explanation could there be as to how he could walk away from his child being choked by her own mother?

I tried to break free from her vise-like hold, but it was no use. She was so strong, and my arms were pinned beneath her weight. Lungs screaming, I desperately tried to suck in air. Beginning to feel faint I looked into my mother's eyes and was chilled to the bone. I saw determination there. This time, she wasn't going to stop. Had I gone too far?

Was this really the way my life would end? Was I going to die?

Then suddenly, she just let go. Even as my oxygen-starved lungs automatically gasped in air, another part of my brain tried to make sense of what had just happened. I knew my mother's expressions. Something had been very different this time. It was a look that told me she would go the distance. So why did she let go so abruptly?

Maybe she'd had a change of heart, but I believed God intervened. Something evil had taken hold of my mother's mind. In my heart, I knew I would have died without His intervention that day.

Mom looked dazed herself, and I managed to get up and stumble into the next room, where I called 911. I told them my mother had tried to strangle me. Within a couple of minutes the same officers that had met with me the night I first reported Mom's abuse were on our doorstep. My heart sank. Weren't there any other policemen in this town?

When they asked me why I'd called 911, I couldn't talk. There was still a tightness in my chest and throat, almost as though something continued to constrict my airway. Tears rolled down my cheeks, but I couldn't seem to produce even one sound.

So Mom spoke instead. She told them about how rebellious I had continued to be and that they didn't know what to do with me. She also accused me of being a habitual liar and would get attention any way I could. Once again, she managed to paint the picture of the concerned mother wanting the best for her daughter.

Finally, I caught my breath and told the police that my mother had tried to strangle me. But once again, they didn't listen. It was obvious they didn't believe me. Instead of being defended, I was told I needed to obey my parents. That I was lucky to live in such a beautiful home with parents who cared about me. The choice was up to me: either behave myself and remain at home or pack my toothbrush in a baggie and they would put me in foster care where I would soon realize how good I had it.

How could they be so cruel? So blind? Why couldn't they see through my mother's act?

Once again I was on my own.

~

As I thought about what God had done for me, literally saving my life, I was convinced about how rebellious I'd become. It was incredibly difficult, but I cut things off with Luis. I hadn't been going to church for a while, but that's where I'd learned about the importance of obeying and honoring your parents. Even though I didn't think *my* parents deserved respect, I decided to try to do things God's way. Keeping my guard up after all they had done to me, I was still getting along with them better than ever before.

I started attending church again and returned to youth group as well. I also got more involved at school and joined a musical. Mine was primarily a dancing role, which thrilled me.

It was the night after our performance, and I was at our cast party. I was laughing along with others at a silly joke when my friend handed me the phone, saying it was my mom. Why would she be calling? I had given her the phone number, but that was just for emergencies. As soon as I said hello she started screaming at me. The whole cast was there to hear every word loud and clear through the receiver. *You're with Luis! I know you are!* She also accused me of drinking, when there wasn't even any alcohol there, insisting I come home immediately. I wanted to disappear.

That did it. All the efforts to be a more obedient daughter went out the window. Being accused of something I hadn't done was so unfair, and my strong sense of justice came to life.

Aware of my friends standing around, I tried to laugh the whole thing off. To act as though it were just one of those silly reactions parents have. But inside I was seething. I wanted to throw things. To take all my efforts of being an obedient daughter and hurl them like so many glass dishes, watching them shatter into a million pieces.

If my parents didn't trust me, I would give them a legitimate reason to withhold their trust. I might as well have fun since I was being accused anyway, regardless of the truth. So I stayed out all night. I wasn't really doing anything bad, but it didn't surprise me when I got home, and my father kicked me out of the house.

I ended up staying with a young woman who liked to party. Within a few days I ran into Luis, and the suspicion that my mother had accused me of became reality; we started to see each other again.

One week before I graduated my mother calmly told me she and my father were getting a divorce. Even though I wasn't getting along with my parents, it was still a shock. After all the years of arguing, why now? Was it because I left? Because there was an empty nest? Was this somehow my fault?

That summer I discovered I was pregnant. I was surprised but happy. However, this time, I wasn't taking any chances. Only Luis would know. Even though I was eighteen and living on my own, I knew my parents would be less than thrilled to discover I was expecting a baby again. I was determined they would not interfere in any way.

My mother stopped by to see me one day and spied my prenatal vitamins. Immediately she went off on me, yelling about my bad choices, and how I would ruin her. But I was prepared. I told her in no uncertain terms that I would never again have an abortion.

She must have believed me because she stopped pressuring me except in one area. My mother insisted that if Dad knew about the baby, he would be just as bad as he was the first time. So I kept my condition a secret.

The pregnancy was very difficult. From the beginning, I started bleeding and had to go on bedrest for several weeks. The nurse said women bled all the time. That even if I miscarried it was nothing I did or didn't do.

But what if? Did something happen when I had the abortion? Was this *my* fault? Was it my parent's fault? I was free-falling into an abyss of swirling darkness. I couldn't handle losing another baby. It felt like I'd had no choice, but what if there was something I could have done to prevent the death of my child?

After a while, the deception began to weigh heavily. Dad and I had been getting along much better, and I hated to keep something so special from him. But what if he reacted like before?

The bleeding returned again in the eighth month of my pregnancy. Keeping it from my father was no longer an option unless I wanted the first inkling that he had a grandchild to be in the hospital gazing through a nursery window. Anything could happen in the next couple of weeks.

Using the phone as a shield, I punched in the number. Our conversation went far better than expected, and he phoned me the next day, inviting me to his home. In a few days, it would be Christmas, but I wasn't in a festive mood. Why did he want me to come *there*? What if he was only pretending to be calm about the pregnancy, and he flew into a rage? He might hurt the baby.

I had to tell myself I was overreacting. To just put one foot in front of the other. When my father opened the door, his eyes swept over my swollen belly. How had he missed it the last time we were together? But I'd worn loose, bulky clothing, and my father had always been a bit unobservant.

Dad gave me a careful hug and handed me a box wrapped for Christmas. Tearing back the paper, the words *camcorder* jumped out. What was going on? From fear of a violent outburst to being given such a thoughtful present, it was hard to adjust. This was like a beautiful benediction, after all we had been through. Now I had a way of recording precious moments in my baby's life.

He also gave me a sweet card. It said something about how a father always wants the best for his daughter—but even when things didn't work out perfectly, they never stopped loving their little girl.

My throat tightened, and I tried to swallow past the lump. Tears rolled down my cheeks in reaction to such tender, uncharacteristic words. Why had I listened to my mom? Why had I waited so long to tell him? Still, now there was a chance for a new beginning and for true restoration.

Five weeks early, I gave birth to an exquisite little girl who we named Elaina. One look at that precious face brought the first true measure of healing to my mama's heart. Although another child could never replace the one I had aborted, for a while, the pain seemed to ease a bit.

Mom and Dad tried to be there for me. I knew they thought eighteen was too young to be having a baby, but this time neither seemed to hold the pregnancy against me.

I was completely in love with my beautiful daughter. I delighted in caring for her. At the same time, I was still so emotionally broken. There were many ways I fell short of the kind of mother I had dreamt of becoming. I was working, going to school, and trying to raise a child the best way I knew how.

When Elaina was only six months old, I discovered I was pregnant again. I was a little overwhelmed at the thought of another baby so soon. I would only be nineteen years old, and I looked even younger. What would people think about an unmarried teenager, with two babies barely a year apart? After talking it over with Luis, we agreed that we should get married. Quickly I began planning a wedding.

At that point, many things were going well in my life. Luis and I had good jobs, and we had purchased our first home. We had nice cars, and I was pursuing my education. On the surface, things looked good. For so long I had tried to prove to my parents that I hadn't made a mistake about Luis. That we were going to more than just "make it." I would show them they had been wrong.

But as I prepared for the wedding my nerves began to fray. I began to feel literally sick to my stomach, and I knew it had nothing to do with the pregnancy. I wasn't excited about becoming Luis's wife. This wasn't how I pictured my wedding would be. But everything had already been paid for, and I had been living with the man for two years by then. It was time.

So I walked down the aisle with a smile on my face, but deep down I knew I was making a mistake.

~

Almost immediately our relationship seemed to change. Or maybe I just began seeing things the way they'd been for quite a while. We started fighting a lot, and it reminded me of how my parents were when I was growing up. The last thing I wanted for my children was for them to constantly hear their parents fighting.

One of the most painful things Luis ever told me was that he loved our daughter more than he loved me. What did I even do with that? I wanted him to cherish Elaina, but once again I was being rejected by someone who once said I was his world. It was like I was stuck on a merry-go-round seeing the exact same scene every time it made a full rotation. Would it ever stop?

Once we brought little Joselyn home from the hospital things got even worse. Elaina wanted nothing to do with me and clung even more tightly to Luis. On one level I knew that was normal when a new baby arrives, but when Luis encouraged her behavior, I was sure I was going to lose her. My heart was breaking, and I began crying over the smallest things. My appetite was gone, and I wished I could sleep for a week. Instead, I had to continue to care for my family and to help provide for them.

~

Adam came home to help me celebrate my twenty-first birthday. It had been years since my brother had been in the area, no doubt avoiding our parents. He took me to a local bar, and once the news got out that I was celebrating my legal drinking age, it seemed as though everyone there wanted to buy me a drink.

As Adam and I began talking about our childhood, I became very emotional. Pretty soon I was crying and couldn't seem to stop. So we left before I made a complete fool of myself.

It probably wasn't the best decision, especially since I'd had so much to drink, but Adam decided to stop at the cemetery to see Aunt Shirley's grave. Shirley had been a good friend of Mom's, but she was so kind to my brothers and me that she was more like an aunt or a second mom. When she was diagnosed with breast cancer and died a few months later, it was devastating to all of us.

Adam had missed the funeral nearly six years earlier, and now he wanted to pay his respects. I found myself sobbing all over again. It was as though I were drowning in an ocean of grief.

In addition, standing next to Adam in that graveyard reminded me of how he had abandoned me all those years before. He had to have known what our mother would be like without him there to protect me, yet he had chosen to leave me to face it on my own. How could he have walked away like he did?

Being beside Aunt Shirley's grave also triggered a memory that had lain dormant within the recesses of my heart. She died less than a year after my abortion. Her death hit so much harder because it made me think about my baby even more. Suddenly as I sobbed in that graveyard, tears dripping down my cheeks unchecked, I recalled the dream I'd had the night after Aunt Shirley's funeral.

I saw Aunt Shirley in a rocking chair. As she rocked back and forth, she looked down with such love at a tiny bundle in her arms. Gazing at the sweet little one, I immediately knew it was my precious baby boy. The one I missed so much.

It was such a comforting dream because I knew that Aunt Shirley had loved Jesus. Surely she was in heaven, and that meant so was my baby.

Still, I was overcome with grief on many levels. My emotions gathered to form the perfect storm. Adam didn't know what to do with me, so he finally scooped me up and brought me back home. Luis came out to the car when we pulled up, and he carried me inside. When he lifted me to his chest, I grabbed his arm, saying, *Luis, I have to tell you something terrible. It's really important. Luis, I had an abortion. I didn't want to, but I aborted our baby.* Then I lay my head against his chest and sobbed.

The next morning, I woke up and remembered what I'd told Luis. In the light of day, I couldn't believe I'd blurted out my secret. Now that he knew I was terrified of what he would say to me.

Soon, Luis came into the bedroom and sat on the edge of the bed. I simply said, "I'm so, so, sorry Luis." A river of tears began to flow again, and Luis gathered me close and let me cry. When I finally had the courage to look in his eyes, I didn't see the anger or judgment I had always dreaded. Only a tenderness that hadn't been evident for a while.

Had he suspected I'd had an abortion all along? He continued to alternately hold me and hug me for several minutes. I was so grateful for his gentleness, realizing there must be some love that remained.
No longer having to hide that painful secret was like finally being able to drop a heavy burden that had been weighing me down for a very long time.

Redeemed

The kindness Luis had shown me didn't last very long. On top of that, it seemed as though my brother's visit had opened Pandora's Box. My past had caught up with me, and there were many things about my present I didn't like either.

In the midst of all the pain and loneliness, I cried out for God to help me. It had been a long time since I had prayed unless there was an emergency. Now, I knew how much I needed Him and wanted to know Him. With all my heart, I begged Jesus to come and save me.

I had no idea what to expect, but almost immediately it was as if a blanket of calm fell over me. There was a sense of comfort too, and of knowing I was no longer alone. My heart was overwhelmed that Jesus would love me, despite all the sin in my life.

Suddenly, I began reading the Bible as much as I possibly could—the words seeming to come alive. I woke early every day before the rest of the family to spend a few precious moments with my Savior. My eyes were opened to the truths buried in Scripture, and I could see that they were for me, personally. I began to experience an intimacy with the Lord that I had never known. I tried to share my love for God with Luis, but he wanted nothing to do with any of it. Still, I began attending church regularly again, this time with my daughters.

Even though I knew Luis and I didn't have the best relationship, my world was rocked when he announced he wanted a divorce. A *divorce*? It was such a shock, especially when he told me a big part of it had to do with the fact that I had become a Christian.

How could this be happening? I tried to get my husband to reconsider. Despite our differences, I felt the best thing for the girls would be for us to stay together. But Luis refused, filing for divorce the very next week.

I couldn't believe it. All my dreams were falling apart, and I searched for a foothold on the slippery slope of my mind. I was caught up in a whirlwind of doubt and confusion. Could the girls and I make it on our own? Would Luis help us financially? Would he fight me for custody?

Once again, I found myself losing weight as my appetite disappeared. I ate only to try to keep my strength up. I couldn't afford to be sick with all that was on my plate. I was utterly depleted. But God was my constant, even when I faltered.

~

Just when I finally believed I could make it on my own, with the Lord as my strength, along came Cory. We were almost instantly drawn to each other. It wasn't simply a physical attraction, although I was definitely pleased with the way he looked. But I was even more impressed by his deep love for the

Lord. He was very passionate about his faith and had a boldness I admired.

At first, I wondered how he would do with my children, but I needn't have worried. The girls absolutely adored Cory. Both of us knew very quickly that we were supposed to be together. Within three months we were standing before a pastor, saying the time-tested words, "I do."

Cory became a wonderful father to my daughters. Just one year later little Joshua was added to our family. I felt incredibly blessed!

Then shortly after my son's birth, I discovered I was expecting again. Cory and I wanted a large family, so we were okay with it being so soon. After finding out I was six weeks along, however, I began bleeding. A trip to the emergency room revealed I was in the process of miscarriage.

It hit me pretty hard. I had already started "making room" in my heart and in my family for this little one. Although it was so tiny, I knew this was already a baby. A boy or a girl, a son or a daughter.

The heartache I experienced was similar to the pain of the abortion, but with one major difference. I wasn't filled with guilt. This wasn't my choice, nor did I need to wrestle with anyone else seeking to destroy my baby's life. This time, I was able to tuck into the Lord as my refuge and strength. He alone knew why this happened, and I surrendered to the fact that He loved me and also cherished this little one. I drew comfort from God even as I grieved the loss of my child.

Within a few more years I gave birth to two more precious little girls. Although I still felt the ache of the two children who were missing from our family, I rejoiced at the blessings God had bestowed on us.

I wish I could say that my relationship with my mother was healed. That she apologized for all the cruelty and that we experienced reconciliation—but that wouldn't be true. I believe my mother knows the Lord and that one day she will be totally healed. But for now, there is much that is still very broken. What caused her to become so abusive? Had she herself been abused as a child? Did she have an undiagnosed mental illness? Or a personality disorder?

I don't know the answer to those questions. But I can say I have been able to forgive my Mom. We have a relationship, and she visits our family from time to time, but I have firm boundaries in place. I would never allow my children to experience what I did growing up.

Dad and I have remained close. In his own way he apologized for the abortion, and the rest I have chosen to forgive as well. Dad still follows the Hindu religion, and I continue to pray for his salvation daily.

Two of the biggest issues that plagued me my whole life were self-condemnation and self-hatred. The abortion served to intensify those exponentially. In many ways, I felt like the worst person on the face of the earth. Even though I fought hard to resist getting the abortion, I still bore the scar of walking through those clinic doors. Then there was my mother's abuse, my brother's leaving me behind, my father pulling away when I became a teenager, and later forcing me to abort, my divorce...the list seemed endless. Each wound piled on top of the other until the weight of it all became unbearable.

Still, the Lord in His mercy provided special moments of healing along the way. One of the most precious gifts I ever received arrived the night of my 30th birthday.

It had been a difficult day, and my heart had been heavy. My family had done so many things to let me know I was loved and appreciated, but there was someone I was missing very much. Finally, I drifted into a beautiful dream.

I was standing in an open clearing with a young man. I immediately knew he was fifteen because I recognized him as my son. It had been fifteen years since he was taken from my body at the abortion clinic.

He looked at me with such love. Then he opened his arms, and I stepped into his embrace. Hugging him close, I was immediately filled with a warmth that bubbled up from within, and I laughed a happy laugh. I couldn't believe how wonderful I felt...I was being held by my son!

He was taller than me by several inches and held me tenderly. He never actually spoke, but somehow I knew he wanted to comfort me. Comfort me! Shouldn't it be the other way around?

But my precious boy was not in need of comfort. He radiated joy and peace. A younger boy ran in circles around the two of us, and now and then flashed a smile my way. Even though he never came over to me, I knew he was the baby I lost to miscarriage.

I have no idea how long I was with my boys, I only know that I had never felt so at peace. So filled with comfort and love.

I awoke the next morning feeling more refreshed than I had been in a very long time—if ever. A sense of calm and well-being enveloped me like a gentle cloud. The sadness I'd felt before falling asleep was gone, and my heart swelled with joy. Now I knew beyond a shadow of a doubt: My boys were very much alive, and I would see them again someday. What a beautiful birthday present!

Even though I will always deeply regret my abortion, I am profoundly grateful for the mercy and forgiveness God has lavished upon me. One of the verses that I've clung to when guilt and shame threatened to overwhelm is Romans 8:1-2, "There is therefore now no condemnation for those who are in Christ Jesus. For the law of the Spirit of life has set you free in Christ Jesus from the law of sin and death." (ESV)

I am overwhelmed by God's mercy and grace in my life. He has given me a husband who not only loves me; he *gets* me. Cory has demonstrated a tenderness towards me that I didn't even know existed. Through his love and incredible patience, I have experienced a deeper level of healing.

Yet, there have still been moments when I've been gripped by fear. Fear that my past would catch up with me. That even though Cory had proven himself to be faithful, someday I would wake up to see him packing his bags and walking away. Abandoning and rejecting me like so many before him.

But when those times come, my husband lovingly reassures me that I have his heart. That he is committed both to our children and to me. Even more that he is committed to the vow he made to me before the Lord. That's when I know he's not going anywhere.

Cory and I also share a passion for reaching out to the brokenhearted, especially to teenagers. I can sense their pain and deep loneliness in ways that many others cannot. Unbelievably, the Lord has taken the very things that once caused me great pain and miraculously used those same wounds to help others with their own source of pain. No matter what someone is suffering, the cure is always the same: the love of Jesus Christ.

It is my great desire that the Lord would take my story to demonstrate how He can redeem even those things in our lives that feel unredeemable. The truth is He is weaving a ribbon of redemption into your life as well. The Bible promises that if you seek Him, you will find Him.

With all my heart I pray that you do.

"You have turned for me my mourning into dancing; You have loosed my sackcloth and clothed me with gladness, that my glory may sing Your praise and not be silent. O Lord my God, I will give thanks to You forever!"

Psalm 30:11-12 (ESV)

Ribbon Reflection

When I met with Layla, her story touched me deeply. She is a beautiful example of God's redeeming love. Although Layla faced tremendous obstacles in her past, as well as repeated rejection and abandonment, today she emanates a sense of peace and joy that is evident to all.

Like Layla, I experienced hardships growing up. My mother had a rare bone disease, and several times a year, she was hospitalized. My dad's work frequently kept him out-of-state, so my siblings and I were placed in homes within the community. It is my belief that the person who "cared for me" during those periods, also molested me.

When something traumatic happens, the mind is capable of suppressing those painful memories so deeply; sometimes the person isn't consciously aware of those events. This was my case.

Although I sensed something traumatic happened to me when I was young, I had nothing concrete to back up that feeling. Still, for years I struggled with fear and anxiety—even panic attacks, despite the fact that it seemed I had the "perfect life," with a husband who loved me and two children we both adored.

One day, several years ago, I was working around my house when I heard the Lord speak so clearly in my spirit, I quickly ran for a scrap of paper to write it down. It's a phrase that will never grow old:

Be brave, Jenny, I will make all things new. Ask, trust, and believe—and see the salvation of the Lord.

For about a year, God was preparing me to remember things that would be hard to face. It was a season requiring courage. Yet once the time was right, although there were certainly moments of intense pain, even fear, I can honestly say that my God has indeed made "all things new."

During those months, I clung tightly to the God Who promised never to leave me or forsake me. I wouldn't trade my healing journey because without it I wouldn't have the freedom I now walk in.

I believe that my past abuse is why I have empathized so deeply with post-abortive women. In part, it's because the majority of women who obtain abortions have also been abused at some point in their life. But the biggest reason is because the abortion procedure *itself* is a violation of body, mind, and soul.

Think about it. The woman is on her back, with her legs in stirrups, while a typically silent, distant male doctor uses instruments to inflict on her the worst pain she's ever experienced in her entire life. Those memories are often branded within in her—a constant reminder of what was done to her.

Have you ever felt as though your past was a bit like the Black Forest? Dark, sinister trees that are pressing up against your back? Perhaps even the branches reaching around to scratch you? The past is not simply your past if it's affecting your present.

If your own journey includes an abortion/abortions or abuse of any kind, I urge you to walk out your healing with someone you trust. During my own healing journey, I met with a wonderful Christian counselor who was of great help to me.

Please look at the section "Where do I go from Here?" at the back of the book for suggestions of where to find help.

I am grateful to say that although the pain of my abuse was difficult to look at, the Lord has done a profound healing in my life. Today, it's as though He burned the "Black Forest" to the ground, and a meadow has sprung up in its place. My past no longer haunts me like it once did.

Although it won't be overnight, I believe God can do the same for you. Your Heavenly Father longs to turn your mourning into dancing, to remove your sackcloth and to clothe you with joy!

Father God,

I lift up everyone reading this book. You long to see them healed and whole. You died to set them free. Will You draw them to Yourself? Give them courage, and the ability to trust that You are good and that You love them with an everlasting love. Help them to call out to You, and find that You are more than enough.

In Jesus's name, amen.

Going Deeper

1. Layla felt trapped in several ways in this story. Describe a time in your life when you felt trapped by your circumstances.

2. There is a common theme of rejection and abandonment by those Layla loved. Do you see an unhealthy pattern repeating itself in your own relationships? Where do you run when these or other negative feelings overwhelm?

3. Although Layla has some very difficult relationships, she also has some healthy ones. Please share which person you are most drawn to, and why. Then tell of someone in your past or present who has been like a lighthouse in the midst of a storm.

Justin's Story

Labeled

I was the black sheep of the family. At least that's what Grandma called me. My parents divorced when I was a toddler, so I only got to go to my dad's place every other weekend. Still, the first time I heard those words as a young boy, I waited till I was with Dad to talk about it.

When Dad explained what the words "black sheep" meant, he had no idea he was defining *me*. Words like "disgrace," "embarrassment," or "someone who doesn't really belong," were added to my expanding vocabulary that day.

Why did Grandma call me that? What had I done? The words were like a branding iron seared into my soul. I didn't want to be a disappointment to my family. I wanted to make them proud. From that moment on, I tried as hard as I could to outrun the label. But somehow, I was never quite fast enough.

My brother Jonathon, on the other hand, was the "golden child." He was good at everything and everyone loved him; especially Mom. Eight years older than me, Ben was the best big brother anyone could have asked for. I wanted to be just like him.

Dad was my favorite person in the whole world. I loved Mom, but I craved being with my father. Whenever we were together, it felt so right, but a handful of days out of the month wasn't nearly enough. When other little boys wanted to be firefighters or pilots when they grew up, I wanted to be a dad.

I wished my father could live with us. Maybe then Mom wouldn't drink so much. She was what people call a "closet alcoholic." She managed not to drink excessively in public, but as soon as she walked in the door, she started in.

I was always cautious whenever I entered the front door, never knowing what I might find. Would she be in her own world? Or would I need to stay out of her way? The bottle was her friend, but it wasn't mine.

Whenever my mother was in "one of her moods," I either tried to be somewhere else or on my best behavior. But many times I couldn't avoid her anger. She would lash out at me or demand that I bring her the belt. I figured most of the time I deserved what I got, but it was the expression of fury and disgust on her face that wounded me far more than any physical pain she inflicted. No matter what I did, I could never seem to measure up.

At least I had my grandparents. Even though there were times when Grandma still called me "the black sheep," I was sure she had her reasons. Both she and Grandpa were kind and loving towards me. They also loved God, and sometimes we went to church with them.

When I was about ten, I went to a Billy Graham crusade. I had already heard about God's love for me but somehow, this time, it really clicked. Billy Graham said I was separated from God because of the bad things I had done, but if I believed Jesus died on the cross to pay for my sin and invited Him to come into my heart, He would. Later, I walked down front and prayed the sincere prayer of a child that night. For quite a while, I remember feeling so clean.

I continued to go occasionally to church with my grandparents, and a few years later, I got involved with the junior high youth group. I loved everything about it. Finally, I found a place where I could be myself and feel accepted. A place where I belonged.

When the first youth pastor left, I was devastated. After that, It was hard to trust someone else quite as easily. Then it happened again.

Why did everyone I got close to decide to leave, only to be replaced by someone else saying how much they cared about me? As if there was a revolving door of potential candidates waiting in the wings somewhere.

Finally, I was done trusting the leaders any more. They said they loved me but never stuck around long enough to prove it. And if they represented God, then I was done with Him too.

Champion

School was a place I exceled. I was very good at sports, especially football. And unlike many of my fellow athletes, I took academics seriously, maintaining a high GPA.

I was fourteen when I started dating Kelly. I didn't go into the relationship lightly. In fact, I remember hoping we would get married someday. My brother was married at nineteen. Since I looked up to him and respected him, I just assumed I would do the same thing. So while other boys were dating a different girl every week, I was far more earnest about my intentions. That was also when I became sexually active. Although I had thought our relationship would last forever, about a year later we broke up.

I was fifteen when I fell head-over-heels-in-love with Hannah. She was strong and beautiful, with long brown hair and brown eyes, and a huge smile that matched her heart. She was kind to everyone, especially to the younger girls who needed a little encouragement.

Hannah was a wonderful athlete. Besides being on the track team, she was also a cheerleader, so it was natural that we would hang out after games. We hadn't been dating very long when we stayed out late one night talking.

I could sense something was really bothering her. After a few minutes, Hannah lowered her head, her voice dropping to just above a whisper. She said that from the time she was six years old her father began molesting her. It had gone on for years, and sometimes she still had nightmares from it all.

I didn't know what to say. For some reason, people seemed to tell me things they wouldn't tell anyone else. But how was I supposed to respond? Hannah wouldn't even look at me anymore, and she was crying. So I put my arms around her and held her close, rocking her back and forth. Once she calmed down I encouraged her to tell her aunt about everything since she was afraid to tell her mom.

Within a day or two her father had been arrested and later sentenced to many years in prison.

Even though her dad's imprisonment was the right thing, it was still a hardship on the family. Pretty soon, everything began falling apart. Hannah's mom, Sarah, was really struggling, trying to hold things together, and her eleven-year-old brother was having a tough time as well.

Hannah struggled with the reactions from others once the news of the abuse became public. On top of that, having to talk to the judge about the case had stirred up memories she longed to forget.

I'd been spending the night since everything about

her dad had come out. She really didn't want me to leave, and in any case, I wanted to be there for her. After a while, it only made sense that I move in, so I didn't have to keep going home to get things I needed. Besides, Mom and I had been butting heads a lot, and not having to come home to her angry, drunken outbursts was a relief.

Now, we could finally settle into a routine of sorts, and hopefully, everyone would begin to heal.

Struggle

One night, in the midst of all the emotional upheaval, Hannah came downstairs with a look of shock on her face. I didn't understand what was wrong until I saw what was in her hand. It was a little white stick with two distinctly pink lines on it.

Hannah started sobbing. Both of us knew we were far too young to have a child. Our futures were in front of us, and a baby would have altered things drastically. Especially for Hannah. Abortion just seemed like the best solution.

I worried about what people would think. My mom would be furious, and what about Dad? The last thing I wanted to do was disappoint him. And what would this do to my plans for a football career?

Hannah had her own worries. Who ever heard of a pregnant cheerleader? And her track would have to go too. Would she have to drop out of school if the pregnancy got too difficult? Besides, she didn't need any more attention than she already had, with everyone knowing about the past molestation and her father's subsequent imprisonment.

Once Hannah told her mom about the pregnancy, she immediately agreed abortion was the only answer. Sarah set an appointment for the next day.

Not surprisingly, I had never been inside Planned

Parenthood. In the back of my mind, I knew it was a place to go for birth control. On some level, I was even aware that they did abortions. But what shocked me was the ease of how quickly everything happened. One phone call, and hours later Hannah was in the waiting room. It was all so surreal.

Sarah and I sat with Hannah as she waited for her name to be called. Her hand was like ice when I reached to hold it. She looked so scared, and I wished I could make things better. Wished she didn't have to be there at all. But how could either of us deal with a baby? We would never be able to reach the goals we had each set for ourselves. I wouldn't be able to provide adequately for the child. And what would my family think if they heard about this? I would never be able to live it down.

Once Hannah's name was called and she was gone, I became restless. I distracted myself by watching the women who were coming out the opposite door. Some of them looked devastated. I assumed they had just had an abortion, and my stomach clenched. *Was that how Hannah would look?*

Others appeared as though they had just gotten their nails done. Had their appointment been for something else? Or did the abortion somehow not affect them like it seemed to affect the others?

About an hour later Hannah came out. She looked so weak and tired—she barely glanced at me. The ride home was very quiet. I was at a complete loss for words of comfort.

After that, Hannah seemed to spiral even more. I didn't know if it was due to the abortion or to all the stuff about her molestation.

Nights were the worst. That was when the bulk of her abuse had taken place since her mom worked the night shift. Hannah would wake up crying and shaking. I tried to console her, wrapping her in my arms. But it was like putting a band aid on a gaping, oozing wound.

It was such an intense time. I was only fifteen, yet had taken on the role of protector and encourager. I was far too young to be a knight-in-shining-armor, and the responsibility began to weigh on me. I remained with the family for a year and a half, trying to hold them together as best I could. But it was as though I couldn't breathe anymore with everyone clinging to me so tightly. My performance at school started slipping.

That's when Dad stepped in. He could see the toll everything was taking and since he knew living with Mom would be even worse, he suggested we look for an apartment for me. He helped me out financially and got me all set up.

Once we weren't with each other 24/7, Hannah and I started to grow apart. Eventually, we broke up. In my mind, I had been sure we would always be together. That we would get married and live happily ever after. I loved her as much as any teenaged boy was capable of loving another human being. Walking away from Hannah was the hardest thing I had ever done.

Striving

Somehow, despite all the upheaval in my private life, I maintained a high academic standing. As the captain of the football team and one of the star players, I was offered a full-ride scholarship at a prestigious university.

I thought I'd finally made it. I joined a fraternity, and for the first time got into the party life-style pretty hard. Drinking was something I swore I would never do. I had watched it destroy my mother, and I'd never wanted any part of it. Watching the players on my football team in high school get wasted reinforced that decision. But now I was breaking all my own rules.

Even my attitude towards women had changed, mainly when alcohol was involved. I had my pick of women, and I looked to them more for pleasure than for a relationship.

One night, I had just had an intimate encounter and was getting comfortable to sleep when I heard as clearly as though it were an audible voice, "Are you done yet?"

My heart started beating fast, and my breath nearly stopped. There was no question in my mind as to Who was speaking. In a flash, I recalled my decision to follow Jesus at the Billy Graham crusade, and the moment at youth group when I felt God calling me into something much bigger than myself. "I called you by name. You have been trying to find happiness in all these things, but you will never find it apart from Me. Are you done running away yet?"

Shaking, I was struck to the core of my being. It was like the Apostle Paul's encounter with God in the Bible. He had been persecuting Christians for years. On his way to having a few more radical Jesus-followers imprisoned or killed, he was temporarily blinded by a very bright light. God stopped him in his tracks. Paul would become one of Christ's most devoted followers and leaders. Later, he would be martyred for his "sin" of sharing the message of Jesus's death and resurrection and everyone's need to surrender their lives to Him.

That's what the Lord did for me that night. He stopped me in my tracks. And just that quickly, I did an 180-degree turn and headed in the opposite direction.

I left the fraternity and started going to church again. After a while, I was approached to become an intern, where I began to study the Bible in earnest and to learn from the leaders of the church. Before I knew it, I was a pastor to young adults. To say that my life changed would be a huge understatement.

Yet even though I was very genuine in my passion to both love and serve God, I was also striving. I was on a treadmill, trying to outrun my past. To somehow become worthy. Even though I was surrounded by people who loved and encouraged me, I knew I was "the black sheep." I knew I had dirty secrets that disqualified me from ever fully gaining God's approval. I could tell others how to find freedom and forgiveness, but somehow I was too nasty and dirty to be completely washed clean. Or to measure up.

It had been five years since I had walked into that Planned Parenthood clinic. The decision that had seemed so right at the time now burned in my conscience. Why hadn't I thought about adoption? My brother had been married for a few years at the time. Due to a prior illness, his wife was unable to have children. Wouldn't they have loved our child as their very own? What if I had said "Let's think about *this*," instead of jumping to abortion as our only alternative?

Part of the reason I couldn't stop thinking about my child was because everywhere I turned I would run into a five-year-old. Walking the halls of my church, a family would stop to greet me. As I knelt down to be eye level with one of their children, I would ask how old they were. "Five." Or I would be in the mall, and I would see an adorable little girl and inquire how old she was. "Five." It happened so many times that I started saying, "Let me guess…are you five?" They always were.

Finally, I called my friend Jason. He had been a good buddy in college. We had traveled similar paths, and he had also become a pastor very early in life. To that point, I had never told anyone my dark secret, but I couldn't hold it in any longer.

Jason, I have to tell you something. Five years ago my girlfriend and I had an abortion.

Once I began I couldn't stop. It all came pouring out, along with my painful questions about what happens to aborted babies and where my child was now.

Jason listened without judgment, then encouraged me to go on a solitary retreat.

Taking his advice, I got away for a couple of days and there I heard from the Lord in a powerful way. In a quiet meditative moment, He told me He would set many others free through my story.

Then I had a dream.

I saw many children laughing and playing. But one child came over to me calling, "Daddy! Daddy!" Before I even heard those words, I knew. This was my child.

For a moment, I just stared, struck dumb at the sight of a beautiful little girl with dark curly hair and dark eyes. She looked like me, but I could see Hannah in her features too. Scooping her up in my arms, she put her arms around my neck, and I was lost. Sobbing and holding her tightly, I just kept saying, "I'm so sorry; I'm so sorry!"

I don't recall if she spoke to me or not, but somehow I knew I was forgiven. Cleansing tears poured down my face, even as an incredible peace flooded my heart. My child was happy. She wasn't suffering. She had even forgiven me!

Then, it was as if I were in a movie and the scene changed. I was in an airport terminal running after an adult Hannah. Trying to get her attention I kept calling her name, but she wouldn't turn around. Instead, she seemed to quicken her pace.

In desperation, I yelled out, "I saw our child. She's okay, Hannah. She's happy."

She must have heard my words because she simply stopped in the middle of the busy airport walkway and began sobbing. Quickly I went over and put my arms around her, trying to give some comfort while we cried together, grieving for the child we both ached for.

After the dream, I was more settled and peaceful. I also realized I needed to contact Hannah. I sent her a message, telling her about the dream and letting her know I believed our child was in heaven.

I apologized for immediately jumping to abortion as our only option the night she came downstairs with that positive pregnancy test. I could have tried to hide behind the whole "it's her body," rhetoric, but now I knew the truth. How I reacted when she told me and how I just sat there in that clinic spoke volumes. I was in full agreement and helped push her to that decision.

I didn't get much of a response. I think it probably took her by surprise. But I pray it helped her along her own healing journey.

I also went to see Mom. She was struggling physically but was happy to see me. I told her I was sorry for pulling away from her over the years. She may not have been a model parent but she was still my mother, and I wanted her to know how much I loved her. We had an amazing conversation. As I shared about what God was doing in my life, right there over lunch, my mom recommitted her life to Christ. I was so thrilled.

It wasn't long after that I received a call from Jonathon. Mom had just had a massive heart attack and was on life support.

At her bedside, looking down at my mother hooked up to all those tubes, my heart grieved. There was so much more I would have liked for us to talk about. To walk through. But now it would have to wait.

One of the things I had never gotten around to telling her about was the abortion. I could never seem to find the right words. Especially knowing how much she would have loved a granddaughter. But in her final moments when I was alone with her, I whispered that her grandchild was waiting for her. I could only imagine Mom's joy at such a meeting.

A few months later, I got another phone call. It was Jonathon again, only this time it was about my father. *No, Lord! Not Dad too!* He had suffered a massive heart attack and died instantly.

At twenty-three years old I lost both my parents within five months. It was a difficult season, and confusing at times. But in the end, I surrendered it all to the One Who loves us and gave Himself for us.

I clung to the truth that someday we would all be together. What a reunion that would be!

Forward

Years had passed. I married the love of my life, and we had a little boy, with another baby on the way. I had been so blessed beyond my wildest dreams, and certainly beyond what I deserved. God was so good.

As a pastor for almost ten years, I'd seen much heartache in my congregation. Broken people in need of healing, not platitudes or pat answers.

Several individuals shared with me about a local ministry called "Wellsprings of Freedom International." It was an inner healing and deliverance ministry based in Rock Island, Illinois. People were coming to me who I knew had been struggling with deep wounds, even addictions, but were now walking in a far greater freedom. They attributed the transformation to the healing of Jesus Christ through prayer sessions at Wellsprings. I was intrigued.

After meeting with Pastor Tim Howard, I decided to take the training class they were offering.

One of the requirements of the training was to "practice" what we'd been learning. How else would we understand how to help others find freedom through prayer sessions if we didn't practice? That evening, it was my turn to be the one in search of healing.

After listening to some worship music, Pastor Tim spoke a prayer covering over our time together. Then he asked me if there was a particular wound in my past that continued to bother me.

Suddenly, I had a clear image in my head of myself sitting on the bed in Hannah's room all those years ago. I could feel the profound sadness that I'd experienced after the abortion. But almost everyone in the room that evening attended the church where I was a pastor. What would they think of me if they knew what I had done?

However, I wanted to heal. I wanted more freedom. So I took a deep breath and told them that when I was fifteen, my girlfriend and I had an abortion.

Tim explained that when something traumatic happens in our life, we can get "stuck" there. That in a very real sense my fifteen-year-old self was still deeply wounded and had not experienced the healing I had found as an adult.

Tim asked Jesus if He would allow me to see Him holding my child. Immediately I saw a baby being held securely against a man's chest. I couldn't see His face, but I was sure it was my Savior.

I was mesmerized. The child had the same dark, curly hair like the one in my dream years before. Then, Tim asked if Jesus would be willing to place the child in my arms. Suddenly my arms were filled with the most precious little baby I had ever seen. I could smell her sweet scent, and feel her soft skin.

I held her, weeping and asking her to forgive me for choosing to abort her all those years before. Then I heard in my spirit, "I'm not angry with you. I've forgiven you."

By that point, everyone in the room was weeping as well. When I was asked if I would like to name her, I immediately knew what it should be. My mom had wanted a little girl very badly. Jonathon and I had heard her say many times if we had a little sister, she would name her Elizabeth. So in honor of Mom, that's the name I chose for my daughter. Somehow it seemed fitting.

Once I handed my child back to Jesus, Tim asked the Lord to pour healing oil into the wound and to cover it with new skin. It's hard to express the depth of healing I experienced in that "practice" session that day. It has literally transformed my life.

~

As a man, I never wanted to admit to myself how much the abortion damaged me. We think we just need to "solve the problem," but there is so much emotional fallout when we make the choice to abort.

I would like to apologize on behalf of all the men who did not stand for life. Who, by not speaking up, making it known that they would be there for their child, put so many women in an awful position; choosing what they never really wanted to choose.

Although I finally know I've been completely forgiven, I'm still very aware that someone incredibly special is missing from my family. Missing from my life. This year, Elizabeth would be turning 16. But she won't be going to prom. I will never walk her down the aisle. Everywhere I look, there are reminders that my daughter isn't with me. Although I have found tremendous healing, I still have the consequences of that decision so long ago.

More than anything, I want to reach people who feel they have been disqualified. Who believe that because of something they have done, or because of a trauma they experienced, they are too damaged or too sinful to deserve God's love and forgiveness.

By that standard, I certainly don't deserve God's love. But that's completely missing the point. The Bible says all have sinned and fallen short of the glory of God. There is no one that is righteous on their own. But praise God, He isn't looking for perfect people, He's looking for people who know they're not perfect! People who know they are sinners in desperate need of a Savior.

Father God,

I pray You would reveal to each man and woman reading

this, that regardless of where they are from, what they have done or how dirty they feel, through Jesus' sacrifice on the cross the penalty for their sins has been <u>paid</u>. May they know they can be completely forgiven and washed clean (1 John 1:9). Remind them of who You are, a Good Father and Loving Savior—waiting to give them life. May they see You and encounter Your Love like never before, confidently walking forward, knowing their past does not define them. Empower them to live boldly and confidently for Your Glory.

In Jesus' name, I pray, amen.

"The thief comes only to steal and kill and destroy. I came that they may have life and have it abundantly. I am the good shepherd. The good shepherd lays down His life for the sheep."

John 10:10-11 (ESV)

Ribbon Reflection

Justin made a remarkable turn-around as a young man. Even so, underneath there remained a festering wound. The Good Shepherd watches over His sheep and tends to their injuries.

There comes a point in our lives when Jesus lets us know if we want to move on from where we are, then we have to let go of whatever is weighing us down.

One of the titles of Justin's chapters is called *striving*. Ever since he was a little boy, he'd been working incredibly hard to change the way people saw him. To prove he wasn't a "black sheep." Then, he and Hannah had an abortion and the struggle to prove he was worthy became even more difficult.

Although Justin was doing many good things for the Lord, in his heart he felt disqualified from ever gaining God's approval. He described that period in his life as being "on a treadmill, trying to outrun his past."

Despite being surrounded by people who loved him and encouraged him, he knew the *truth*. He was the black sheep. He could help direct others to find forgiveness from their past, but he felt his own stain was so deep that it could never be completely clean.

BUT GOD. I love how God actually pursues us. His amazing grace is not only available to us all, but He continues to knock on the door of our heart long after the moment we first believed. The truth is, we never stop needing a Savior.

When we wander from the fold, He continues to be our Good Shepherd and goes in search of us. Jesus longs for us to ask Him for what we need and to trust His heart. To believe that He loves us and longs to give good gifts to His children.

One of the most beautiful gifts He gives us is when He speaks to us. Although He communicates most often through His Holy Word, He also speaks directly to our hearts in that unmistakable voice.

For Justin, "Are you done yet?" were life-changing words that turned his world upside-down. They triggered a profound repentance in his life. Jesus also used a dream to allow Justin to see his child and find a measure of healing. Then later, a vision during a prayer session, where he held his baby and experienced incredible peace and the ability to be finally able to forgive himself.

The truth is, there is no limit to the lengths the Good Shepherd will go to rescue His children. But we need to be listening ... to be paying attention. Are you willing to allow God's healing touch in your own life?
His arms are open wide.

Going Deeper

1. Justin was very young when he found himself wearing a label he didn't like.
a. Can you think of a name or an attitude early in your life that became part of how you defined yourself?
b. Is that "label" still impacting you? In what ways do you see that playing out in your life?

2. Before reading Tom and Justin's stories, did you realize how deeply abortion can affect men? How does that fit with the idea that it's "her body, her choice?"

3. I love the part of Justin's story when everywhere he looks he meets another five-year-old and that soon after he dreams of his aborted child. God obviously pursued Justin to help him find healing.
a. How does that impact the way you see God?
b. Can you look back and trace moments when you sense God was at work in your own life?

Sam's Story

Shaken

I grew up with loving parents in a small country town. I was the baby, with a sister considerably older and a brother four years my senior. Because I was the youngest and the last to leave home, I was given a lot of freedom as a child.

When I was young, Mom was very attentive. We played games together, and I especially loved our times when she would read to me. Dad was quiet but always kind, and he worked hard to provide for our family.

If my parents lacked anything in how they raised me, it would be an awareness of just how bad things could be, even in a sleepy little town.

My grandmother lived close to us, and I loved visiting her. She was quite serious much of the time but had a wonderfully dry sense of humor. Early on, I learned to look for the twinkle in her eyes. For example, when I was little, she handed me a small container with a plastic spoon telling me to go dig my way to China. She never even cracked a smile, but inside I knew she was laughing.

Sometimes Grandma invited me to spend the night with her. That was especially exciting because we usually went fishing at a nearby pond. For lunch, she would pack us her famous peanut butter and butter sandwiches, along with iced tea. Even if I

181

didn't catch anything, I always enjoyed the quiet time with Grandma.

I was eleven years old when I came home from school one day to find Mom crying. Mom almost never cried. Something had to be very wrong because Dad was home in the middle of the day.

When Dad told me my grandmother was dead, I knew there had to be some horrible mistake. It couldn't possibly be true. I had been at her house only two days before, helping her to plant flowers. I was going back tomorrow to finish up.

But my parent's eyes told me they were serious, and suddenly I couldn't handle being in that living room a minute longer. The walls seemed to be closing in on me—I had to get out of there. Had to breathe. Running out of the house, I heard Dad saying, "Let her go."

Later, I learned the awful details. Even now it's hard to accept. Grandma died suddenly of a heart attack. There was no warning—one day she was there, vibrant and alive, and the next she was gone. In just a moment, my whole world came crashing down.

I'm not sure at the time if I realized how profoundly her death affected me. In hindsight, I can see my way of viewing the world radically changed. Suddenly, I understood there were no guarantees that the life I knew would be there tomorrow. From that point on I thought about life only in the present or very near future. Long-term plans wouldn't make sense to me for years to come.

We moved into Grandma's house to save money. It was strange to live amongst her things without her there. It was also hard to see a lot of her belongings removed in order to make space for all of our stuff.

My cousin, Penny, lived about a half-mile away. She was a year older than me but far older in the ways of the world. She was also very disrespectful to her mother, calling her names and refusing to do things she'd been asked to do. No matter how rebellious I would become in later years, it was a rare occurrence for me to raise my voice in disrespect to my parents.

It was Penny who first introduced me to some bad habits. I was only ten when we spiked our hot chocolate with peppermint Schnapps. At thirteen I started smoking cigarettes, and by the time I was fourteen I was smoking marijuana on a regular basis.

I was surprised that Mom never seemed to recognize Penny's influence on me. I remember wishing my mother would suggest that she and I spend more time together, just the two of us.

Instead, she took a painting class and loved it. The next thing Dad and I knew she was either furiously painting something, or going to art shows to sell her work. I was happy for her—that she found something she loved to do. Still, deep down I missed her. Instead of spending extra time together she was gone even more, and my playground continued to be unsupervised.

Then the rug was pulled out from under my "dysfunctional normal" when we had to move. My father got a new job, so my parents wanted to be closer to his work. But what about me? I would have to go to a new school and wouldn't have any friends. It wasn't fair.

I started going to a nearby park where I would smoke and basically sulk. There I met some other teenagers, and soon I was going to their homes to hang out. I desperately wanted to be liked and to belong.

On my fifteenth birthday, I had my first sexual encounter. It actually happened while we were hanging out in my basement with my mom just upstairs. I wish I could say that it was his idea, but I was the one who had suggested it. I remember wanting to experience everything I could before I died. Life just seemed so temporary.

I met Marcia at school the same year. She was smart and sarcastic. Her parents were wealthy, and she lived in a beautiful home. She also had lots of emotional issues, and I think she liked having me around so I could listen to her problems.

After school, we often went to her house to do homework. She saw herself as my academic savior. It wasn't as if I were stupid, although that's exactly what Marcia said I was on more than one occasion. But if I was struggling in a particular subject, she always seemed to know the answer. Since she was certain to bring up my lack of knowledge at some point, I often regretted asking for help.

Still, she was funny, and I liked hanging out with her. There were times when the wall between us dropped, and she was more normal. I really liked her then. At other moments, I knew if I truly respected myself, I would walk away from the friendship.

Stolen

A few months later, another girl from school, Staci, invited me to a party she was throwing. She wasn't a super close friend, but I liked parties, so I went. The only catch was she really wanted me to go out with her brother, Todd. I guess he'd seen me around and thought I was cute. That would've been cool, except I wasn't really attracted to him. On the other hand, one of Todd's friends at the party definitely caught my attention.

His name was Joshua. He had a slight build and was about medium height, but he had long blond hair and the most beautiful blue eyes.

Joshua caught me looking at him and smiled at me, and that broke the ice. He had a very nice smile. All night, if Todd tried to monopolize my attention, I would somehow manage to make my way over to Joshua. He didn't give me a huge amount of attention, but I could tell he kind of liked me too.

Later that night, one of the girls said Joshua was considered a "bad boy" by some of the parents. He was a couple of years older than me and came from a poor family. She said his father was often out of work, and that Joshua seemed to have difficulty keeping a job as well. I didn't care about any of that. Didn't she have anything better to do than gossip?

Afterwards, I was thrilled when Joshua asked if I wanted to hang out. That night we stayed up late, talking for hours. He was so easy to be with if I ignored the butterflies in my stomach.

Before I knew it, we were inseparable, spending almost all our free time together. We would either hang out at a friend's house or go to his place.

One night, when Joshua's parents were gone, things got pretty heated. After that, sex became part of what we did when we were together. For me, it wasn't just sex. I was crazy about Joshua and gave him my heart as well as my body.

Joshua was very thoughtful and sweet. But there was one thing about him I didn't care for at all. He lied. Oh, not about terrible things. More like "little white lies," but they made me mad all the same.

For example, once he told me he couldn't hang out, because his parents needed him to help them with something. Later I found out he'd been out with a group of his friends instead. Why did he feel the need to lie about it? And if he was willing to lie about those things, how could I trust him on the really big things? Still, I was crazy about him and willing to overlook his flaws.

Near the end of the summer my breasts felt sore, and when I thought back, I realized I'd missed at least two menstrual cycles. Although I wasn't always regular, I never skipped more than a month.

My mouth went dry, and my pulse began racing. I couldn't be pregnant. That wasn't even on the list of possibilities. Of course, I knew how these things worked; it just couldn't happen to me.

I was freaking out at school when I decided to confide in Sandy. She was a friend who had always been kind to me; there was just something about her I was drawn to. For one thing, she was very open about her faith in God—as though He were a close friend. I loved that she never acted like she was better than anyone else, and it was obvious how much she cared about other people. The bottom line was I knew I could trust her to keep my secret. I also knew that she would pray for me. Prayer wasn't really my thing, but I needed all the help I could get.

Later, when I was at my locker, Sandy came up and handed me a note with a smile and a quick hug. As she walked away, I opened it.

Sam, hang in there! I know a pregnancy sounds scary, but something will work out. I will be praying. If you need anything, call me! Love, Sandy

Quickly stuffing it in my pocket, I headed home.

The next day, Mom found the note in my pants pocket. She really lost it. She took me straight to a clinic, and when the test showed positive, she immediately insisted I have an abortion.

The word hit me like an explosion. What? An *abortion*? That had never entered my mind. Everything was spinning out of control so fast, and I was grasping for something to hold onto.

Mom kept trying to get me to see all the things I would miss out on if I were to have a baby. All the parties and dances at school. All the fun. But when she asked, "Who's going to take care of it? Me?" I didn't know how to answer her.

When I wouldn't immediately agree to the abortion, my mom's anxiety escalated to the point that she began vomiting. That really scared me. It triggered an even greater anxiety in me and the next thing I knew I was covered in hives.

My dad was quiet as usual. But his position was clear—abortion was the only solution. It was like finding out that not only was I outnumbered, but I was on the losing team.

What hurt the most was when Joshua agreed I needed to get an abortion. Secretly, I had wished he would want the baby. Somehow, we would make it work. Instead, he only thought of himself. He didn't want to be saddled with a baby. He never asked me what I wanted. Didn't he care about what this would do to me? To my body? To my heart and mind? Didn't he care about the baby?

Once he made his wishes known, Joshua was noticeably absent. Although, to be fair, it would have been harder to see each other at that point. From the beginning, my parents didn't like him much, and once the pregnancy was revealed, they insisted I never see him again.

I called Marcia to tell her about the pregnancy, hoping to get some empathy for my situation. Instead, she said I would be crazy to try to have a baby at fifteen. How would I ever take care of it? I didn't know the answer to that, but I knew abortion wouldn't be right. Why wouldn't anybody listen to me?

The next morning, Marcia and Penny were at our front door. Not for a nice little visit, but rather a let's-convince-Sam-that-she-needs-to-wise-up-and-do-the-right-thing visit. Mom had asked them over to talk some sense into me.

"Sense"? What part about getting rid of my baby made sense?

They all ganged up on me, immediately shooting down all my objections. They insisted it wasn't a baby at all...just a clump of cells. That didn't sound right, but I was so tired of it all. I couldn't fight it anymore. Without anyone on my side, I finally caved.

With all the stress, I'd been smoking a lot more

cigarettes, one right after another. Anything to try to calm down. Marcia said I was lucky I wasn't throwing up all the time or smoking wouldn't taste very good.

What a word to use—*lucky*. What about any of this could be considered lucky? I wouldn't have minded even being super sick if it meant I could have kept my baby.

Although both my parents knew I smoked, it had been an unspoken agreement that I would never light up in front of them. We were sitting in the living room after Penny and Marcia left. I had agreed to the abortion, and my parents both reached for another cigarette at the same time.

"Well, now can I at least smoke around you guys?" My dad just blinked at me for a few seconds, then he nodded. Immediately I pulled out a cigarette and lit it, drawing deeply on the end, blowing out a cloud of smoke.

It felt so strange—like the most bizarre deal ever struck. The freedom to smoke in front of my parents, in exchange for my baby's life.

~

The next day, my mother drove me to a clinic in a nearby city. Marcia came too, but she and Mom stayed outside the waiting room while I sat by myself. I stared at the beige cinder block walls and the old beat-up furniture, wondering if the other girls in the lobby were waiting to have abortions too. No one made eye contact with anyone else. Every time a name was called I flinched inside, dreading the time when it would be my turn.

Finally, they called my name. I wanted to hide—just become invisible and walk out of the place undetected. But I didn't have any super hero abilities, and what would I do then? There was nowhere for me to go.

I was taken back by a woman in scrubs. I don't remember exactly what I asked her, but even though I would have been about twelve weeks along, she assured me "the pregnancy" was just a blob of tissue. Nothing to be concerned about.

Once I was in the procedure room, I was shocked that the nurse in the room was noticeably pregnant. She spoke kindly to me, but the physician never even looked me in the eye. The only time he spoke was when he told me he was turning on the suction machine, and then as he was leaving, he said I would have some pain and bleeding. He had just touched my body in such a violent and intimate way, yet he remained completely detached. It was like I wasn't even there. To him, I was merely a body—a receptacle to be emptied.

~

I don't remember much about the drive home, except when Marcia leaned over to ask me if "it" hurt. I wanted to scream, "Yes! It was excruciating! The whole thing was far worse than I'd imagined."

But somehow the words got stuck. What would be the point of telling them, anyway? It wouldn't change anything.

When we got home, all I wanted to do was crawl into bed and pull the covers over my head. To pretend it had all been a terrible nightmare. But something began rising up within me, like a tidal wave. *Dear God, what had I just done?*

The nurse had said there wasn't anything really there. Only some "tissue." But really, wasn't that what I'd learned in science class? That all human bodies are made up of cells? Of tissue and fluid?

Now that it was too late I could no longer swallow the lie. If I hadn't gone to that clinic, within about six months, I would have given birth. Then a thought hit me so hard I could hardly take a breath.

Where was my baby? Clearly, it was gone, but gone *where*? We didn't really go to church, although I had been there a few times. I remember hearing there were two possibilities of where people went after they died: heaven or hell. What if that were true? After what I had just done, I thought there was a very good chance I would go to hell when I died. But

193

I desperately needed to know that my baby was in heaven.

I didn't want to ask Mom. Didn't want to cause her more pain. True, she had been the one to push for the abortion. A part of me was very angry at both my parents, but I was angrier with myself. *I* was the one who had gotten pregnant. Ultimately it was my fault.

Still, I *had* to know. With all the courage I could muster, I went to find her. She was in the kitchen peeling potatoes for supper. Such a normal thing to do on a day that had been anything but normal. When I entered the room she looked up, eyes widening. All that crying must have done some damage. I waited for a few seconds, unsure of how to even phrase the question burning inside me. Finally, I blurted out, "Mom, is my baby in heaven?"

For a moment, it was as though time stood still. She just stared at me, blinking a few times. The air pulsed with the question hovering between us. What was she thinking? Why wouldn't she answer me?

Then her face seemed to relax, and all she said was, "Yes."

That was to be the only word she would ever say about my baby. From that moment on we never spoke of my abortion again.

Shattered

Gradually, my body healed. My heart was a different story. I sunk in the quicksand of guilt and shame, hating myself. It was my fault my child had to die. It was the punishment I deserved. If I hadn't had sex, there wouldn't have been a baby to begin with—a baby whose life was snuffed out before it had a chance to begin.

I tried so hard to move on. Somehow, I had to forget what had happened. If only it were that simple.

My mother assumed I would continue to be sexually active and made sure I got on birth control. It may have prevented future pregnancies, but it did nothing to protect my heart.

I still saw Joshua, but everything was different. When I was around him, it only reminded me of everything that had happened. Why hadn't he protected me? Why hadn't he defended his child, instead of demanding its death? He never even asked me how I was doing. Ever. He just picked back up without skipping a beat, as though nothing had happened.

Even as a part of me wanted nothing to do with him, the other part clung to Joshua like never before. I was demanding of his time, becoming quickly angered if he made excuses about why he couldn't be with me. As though I were someone else, I stood

195

by watching myself choke the life out of our relationship.

I hated being alone. On my own, thoughts swirled like a tornado gathering strength, descending with a fury. All the "what ifs and if onlys" collided, intent on destruction. If Joshua was busy, I made sure I had a back-up plan. I was almost never home, even sneaking out in the middle of the night. I would go meet up with friends and walk around town or go hang out at someone's house.

Staying out half the night didn't lend itself to the ability to focus, so skipping school became a pattern. The truth was, sitting at a desk listening to a history lecture or being asked to memorize mathematical formulas made zero sense anymore. How was that ever going to help anything? I was strictly on survival mode.

Mom frequently got phone calls from counselors asking about my whereabouts. I'm sure that really bothered her, but nothing she or my father said or did made much difference. I had my own car, and they never took it away from me. I was like a speeding train off its tracks. Although I know they loved me and worried about me, they had no idea how to help.

Joshua and I continued dating off and on for a year. The first time we broke up, it was over a girl. He swore he didn't do anything with her, but I heard it differently. After a while, I was the one who forgave him and started back up all over again. Deep down I knew Joshua wasn't good for me, but I couldn't let go. Somehow my heart was still entangled.

I kept thinking I could somehow fix him. But the more I tried to get him to do the things I wanted him to do, to *be* the person I wanted him to be, the more he ran in the opposite direction. I was no longer fun for him. It was like we were in the ocean and I was drowning. Latching onto Joshua, I clung to him so tightly he started to go under too.

A year after our abortion, we broke up for good. The final blow was when, once again, he cheated on me. That time he swam away and left me floundering in dark waters.

In my heart, I knew it was for the best...how had we thought we could play in an adult world and not get burned?

~

After that, I started hanging out with my partying friends more than ever. I began to consume larger amounts of alcohol and drugs. Anesthesia, to keep the memories at bay. This time, I even experimented with cocaine and crystal meth.

Unbelievably, I never seemed to become truly addicted. I just preferred to be in an alternate state of mind. I didn't like reality much. I didn't like myself, for that matter.

During my junior year, I dropped out of high school. I began to realize if I didn't make some changes, things wouldn't end well. Although my parents were disappointed I was quitting, in a way, I think they were relieved. At least Mom wouldn't get any more phone calls about her delinquent daughter. I found a full-time job and things started to settle down.

By the time I was eighteen, I finally began looking toward the future. I even started to think about what I could do to advance in my job. Ambition was foreign to me, but it felt good.

That's when I started dating Michael. I had known him for a couple of years, but since he wasn't much of a partier, our paths hadn't crossed very often. Still, he intrigued me. He was kind and funny, and I felt good when we were together.

Michael was probably the first guy to ever genuinely care for me. He made me feel special, although I really didn't know what to do with his affection. How did I deserve such a wonderful man? A few months later, we moved in together, and at nineteen I discovered I was pregnant.

In the beginning, I was pleased—even a little excited. I had hoped we would someday have a child together. The truth was I had longed for a baby ever since my abortion.

But soon my mind was like a toxic waste dump. *What were you thinking? You'd make a terrible mother. You of all people don't deserve a baby! It would only end up suffering from a mother like you!*

My biggest confusion was how I could allow this child to live when my first child was dead.

Completely beaten down by my own thoughts, I told Michael I didn't think we should have the baby after all. I wasn't ready. I wasn't cut out to be a mother. But he refused to give up on me. He said he believed in me, that he knew we could do this.

Finally, I told him about the abortion. I had to. Otherwise, none of my behavior would've made sense. One minute I wanted the baby, the next I wanted an abortion.

I couldn't look at him while I talked, barely speaking above a whisper. The weight of what I had done was overwhelming. Would he walk away now that he knew what I was capable of? I couldn't imagine he would still want me to be the mother of his child.

Instead of being angry or disgusted, he just held me tightly as the floodgates opened and all the pain and shame came pouring out. He told me he loved me more than ever and that we would get through this together. That I was going to be a wonderful mother.

With all Michael's support, I felt I had to try. So, before I knew it, I was going to prenatal visits and picking out baby furniture.

Even though I had made the decision to continue the pregnancy, the abortion was never far from my mind. Sleep became elusive, and I started having nightmares.

It was always the same.

I walked down an alley. It was quite dark, yet at the same time, everything was starkly visible. Approaching a metal dumpster against an old brick building, a cardboard box rested on top, with a small child huddled within. With tiny arms wrapped tightly around its legs, the little one appeared to be shivering.

As I got closer to the dumpster the child looked right at me, and I knew — this was the baby I had aborted. Arms reaching towards me I stepped closer, intending to lift the babe into my arms.

Then the scene began rapidly changing. As I watched in horror, the child began to take on a skeletal-like appearance. Panic began to build, along with a sense of hopelessness and dread. Somehow I knew death was inevitable. Straining towards my child, I tried desperately to take hold of the little arms that reached for me. But suddenly the small body seemed just to melt away, leaving nothing for me to grasp.

Eyes flying open, I would wake suddenly, shaking and sobbing. Michael would hold me tight, trying to comfort me. But nothing could take away the sense of empty arms that lingered throughout the day.

Despite the nightmares, I made it through the pregnancy and delivered a little boy. We named him Jacob. I had a difficult labor and ended up having a Cesarean-section. I don't know what we would have done without Mom's help. We actually stayed with her so she could take care of the baby and me once Michael returned to work. I was in a great deal of pain and found it hard to move. It was such a relief to have Mom handle everything. I believe a measure of healing took place between us during that time. Watching her fall in love with my son was a precious sight.

I had a more difficult transition. Any attempt to comfort or nurture my baby seemed strange. Deep down I felt so undeserving—the old messages of unworthiness continuing to disturb me.

Throughout it all, Michael was wonderful. Once we were finally back home, he was the one who got up in the middle of the night to feed or comfort our child. After watching my husband with our son, I gradually relaxed and was able to care for my baby as well. A few months later, I walked down the aisle to marry the man who had my heart.

Still, I couldn't seem to stop torturing myself. There were times I would rehearse every detail of the abortion. Or I would look up details about fetal development. Somehow I believed it was my responsibility to punish myself.

~

A couple of years later, I stumbled across a Christian radio station. Every time I listened to the music, I felt a pull, a yearning for something more. There were different speakers throughout the day, and I began tuning in to hear them as well. The way they talked, you would think they really *knew* Jesus—personally. It was both mysterious and intriguing.

One day, I turned on my radio and found myself listening intently. The man was saying we were all lost, and that Jesus came to seek and to save us. That really resonated with me. He said Jesus had purposely come to give His life for us. All we needed to do was to put our trust in His death on the cross for our sins, and we would be washed whiter than snow.

How I wanted that! Right then and there I bowed my head and gave my heart to Jesus. I felt such a peace fall on me that day—even a sense of happiness that I hadn't felt in a long time.

I began to change. I quit drinking alcohol and eventually stopped smoking too. I started going to church on Sundays and also joined a Bible study that met twice a week. There were internal changes as well.

Michael wasn't sure what to make of the new me. At first, he probably thought I'd gone off the deep end. At the same time, he couldn't help but notice the new calm I was experiencing, or how I didn't get down nearly as much. In time he adjusted and came to believe it must be good for me and didn't begrudge the time spent in pursuit of my newfound faith.

Giving birth to my second child was drastically different than my first. For one thing, I had already resisted getting another abortion, so that wasn't even a question. I didn't have as many fears either, and I didn't worry about my ability to parent nearly as much. I had a new fledgling relationship with Jesus and a greater peace than I had ever known. I had begun to "cling to the rock that was higher than I was." (Psalm 61:2, paraphrased)

The circumstances surrounding Andrew's birth were difficult. Our baby boy had an infection, and they kept him in the NICU even after I was discharged. There wasn't a place for mothers to stay, so I slept on the couch in the waiting room in order to breastfeed him. I only left briefly to shower. Five days later, he was finally released.

Although it was hard, the time I devoted to caring for my baby forged a solid bond so much sooner than with Jacob. My walk with Christ enabled me to cope with challenges in a new way, and my confidence as a mom continued to grow.

~

One day, after turning on the radio, a woman named C.J. Payne was talking. She was the executive director of a new pregnancy center in town and was inviting anyone struggling with a past abortion to come in for help. It seemed as though every time I turned the radio on, there she was. I knew the Lord was telling me that He wanted me to get some help, but I resisted. No way was I going to tell anyone about something so private and shameful.

One evening, I was attending a home Bible study. Sitting on the couch I glanced down, noticing a newspaper sitting on the coffee table. It was during the Summer Olympics, and my eyes were drawn to the photo of a beautiful young woman who had won a gold medal. She wore a huge smile of victory. Right beside the story was a much smaller article, reporting that President Clinton had approved the use of RU486 for chemical abortions.

Seeing the picture of this young woman, so full of life, beside the article announcing legalized death, broke something within me. I began sobbing, and I couldn't stop.

The other women tried to comfort me, but of course, they had no idea what was going on. Finally, I couldn't hold the secret for another minute. I told the group about my abortion.

To my surprise, they received the news very lovingly. Where I had anticipated judgment, there was only compassion.

I came home that night and told Michael everything. Even though I had shared about my abortion when I was pregnant with Jacob, my ongoing, day-to-day struggles with guilt and shame had remained hidden.

Once again I was reminded of why I loved this man. He immediately encouraged me to go to the center for help. That support meant so much and helped me to be brave.

Around the same time, I found a book called *Tramp for the Lord*, by Corrie ten Boom. One of the chapters was about living in the light, about being honest and walking in the truth. Up until that time, I had been so accustomed to hiding, but now I found myself craving the light. I sensed the Lord leading me to lift those things that had been hidden in the darkness and to expose them. For years I had believed I could never admit my terrible secret—that if anyone discovered my past abortion, they would hate me. But when I opened my very soul to those women and survived, I finally had a taste of the freedom that results from living in the light of God's love.

Later I attended a post-abortion healing bible study, *Forgiven and Set Free*. Being with other women also working through the pain of abortion brought me to a new level of freedom. More of the isolation and self-condemnation lifted. Gradually I was learning to receive the forgiveness and grace offered so freely. It was not an easy process, but it was *good*.

Part of the healing process for the class involved asking God to reveal the gender and name of our child. As I sat quietly before the Lord, I sensed my aborted baby had been a girl. I named her Grace Anne, in honor of the amazing grace that God had extended to me.

By the end of the study, I wasn't completely healed—not by a long shot. No one waved a magic wand and made all the pain disappear. Still, I now had a freedom I'd never experienced before. The leaders told me I would still struggle, and they were right. But I had been given tools that helped me cling to the light when the darkness descended. No longer would I punish myself for sins that Jesus had already died for. I was forgiven and on my way to finding healing and wholeness.

After that, I believe I became a better mother. I could

truly love my children without all the guilt that had shrouded my relationship with them. Things between Michael and I changed, too. For years, I hadn't been able to believe that his love for me was genuine. I had kept him at a distance, protecting my heart. Now that I trusted him more, I began treating him with the love and respect he deserved, and our relationship began to heal as well.

Michael had been watching my transformation, and he knew God was at the root of it all. He decided he wanted what I had experienced, and he surrendered his life to the Lord. What a joy it was to see my husband drawing near to Jesus and finding his own freedom in Christ.

I began praying that I would be blessed with a daughter. The desire came from deep within, and I started to believe it was the Lord Himself who had placed it there.

About a year later, I gave birth to a little girl. We named her Bethanna, which means "from the house of God's grace." I felt so blessed. To say I was overjoyed would be an understatement! As I lovingly cared for my precious daughter, I experienced an even greater freedom, the freedom to enjoy each moment for what it was—a gift. The shadows of guilt continued to diminish.

Three years later, I began volunteering at the same

pregnancy center where I had taken part in the post-abortion healing classes. Eventually, I began leading a class of my own to help others find the peace and freedom I had found.

During a particular class, as I was encouraging the other women to ask the Lord to speak to them about their child/children lost from abortion or miscarriage, the Lord gave me a beautiful vision:

A lovely young woman knelt on a stone floor. She was beautiful, with long, straight brown hair. Wearing a simple white gown, she knelt beside someone, washing their feet. A look of profound joy and peaceful contentment radiated from her.

As I stared at this girl, I immediately knew that she was the child I had once aborted. At that moment, I understood my daughter was happy where she was. She wasn't lonely. She wasn't suffering.

I will always be incredibly grateful to the Lord for pulling back the curtain separating the two of us, and allowing me a peek into Grace Anne's life. It was such a tender portrayal of my heavenly Father's love for me and of His extravagant mercy.

The Lord knew I would need that special touch from Him to strengthen me for what was to come. A short time after my vision, I learned my mother had cancer. We knew she might only have a few remaining months.

What bitter-sweet days we shared together, savoring the moments. Although I hated to watch the toll cancer took on my mother and the pain she endured, I treasured the time we shared.

Since Mom's death, I've experienced gut-wrenching sadness, trying to adapt to a world without her in it. Grieving requires the passage of time and can't be rushed. Yet because of my faith in Jesus Christ, I have the assurance I will one day see her again in heaven.

Mom and I never got around to speaking about the abortion before she died, but I had long since forgiven her. The Lord had given me much peace in the last few years, as I embraced His freedom and forgiveness.

In a sense, I had come full circle. The only words my mom and I exchanged after my abortion was the gut-wrenching question I had to ask that day: "Is my baby in heaven?"

Mom's response had been affirmative that day. But the vision the Lord gave me of Grace Anne had erased any lingering doubts in my mind. I knew that grandmother and granddaughter were now together.

I wait with joy-filled expectation to one day be united with them both.

"The Spirit of the Lord GOD is upon me, because the Lord has anointed me to bring good news to the poor; He has sent me to bind up the brokenhearted, to proclaim liberty to the captives, and the opening of the prison to those who are bound..."

Isaiah 61:1 (ESV)

Ribbon Reflection

Sam's story was heartbreaking. Although she had been tremendously pressured to abort, immediately she took the shame and guilt upon herself. For years the "chains" of shame and guilt, coupled with fear, weighed her down. She was left cowering in the darkness, trying to hide.

When I was thirty-one, my mother was killed by a drunk driver. At that point in my life I was already struggling with fear and anxiety, but losing my mom in such a violent, tragic way, sent me into a tailspin.

Depression made it difficult to get out of bed in the morning, and if not for the fact that I had young children dependent on me, I probably would have sunk even further into hopelessness and despair.

About a year after my loss, I had a dream.

I was in what appeared to be a medieval prison. Sitting on a cold, stone ledge, my hands and feet were in chains. The cell was small and empty, apart from the stone slab that served as my bed. The air was heavy with dampness, the odor foul.

Across my cell was a door with metal bars. I could see an area where there might be a guard on watch, but looking out I saw no one.

At the end of a long corridor, there was a large, thick door. To my amazement, it was slightly ajar, and light was pouring through the thin opening. Somehow, I knew Jesus was just outside the door and was beckoning for me to come to Him.

Looking down at my hands, it was now evident that the chains weren't actually locked, and neither were the shackles on my feet. Glancing at the door to my cell confirmed my suspicion—it was standing open just a bit.

That's when I knew. I could escape.

But somehow, I couldn't make myself move. Fear held me fast; a sense of dread making it almost impossible to think. What would happen if I opened that door and stepped out? What if someone was just waiting to attack?

My heart beat faster, even as I tried to shake the cobwebs out of my mind. What was wrong with me? I wanted to leave ... and go to Jesus—wanted to finally escape all the darkness. I even heard His voice calling me.

But I was afraid. The unknown held me bound.

Can you relate? There are times in our lives when we hear Christ calling us to greater freedom. But we are afraid.

Jesus is calling all of us to *be brave*. He wants us to

come out of the shadows of the things that have held us bound, even though our legs might be a bit wobbly. He's calling us to take a step of faith.

I pray that the Lord will give you the courage to put the first foot forward towards freedom, today. I am praying for you!

Going Deeper

1. In Sam's story, the sudden death of her grandmother caused her to feel as though life was very uncertain. That view deeply affected her future decisions. Think of a time in your life when something happened that altered the way you saw things. Please share the circumstances surrounding that time, and where you are in the process of healing.

2. When Sam faced her second pregnancy, she nearly aborted again because of her sense of unworthiness and shame. Please share about a time when you sabotaged, or was tempted to sabotage, something good in your life because of past wounds.

3. Sam's story reveals the Lord's ribbon of redemption in the midst of her circumstances. Trace the times when God clearly "stepped into" her life to point her in the right direction. Then discuss times when you've seen that to be true in your own life.

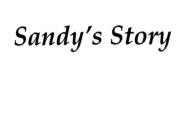

Sandy's Story

Innocent

Growing up I never doubted I was loved. My parents were both affectionate, and there was always laughter in our home. Dad was a mechanic and owned a gas station in town. Mom stayed at home, taking good care of me.

I had been the only child for two years when Doreen arrived. I don't really remember anything before her, and as far as I was concerned, she was my very own living, breathing baby doll. In fact, I called her Dolly Baby, a name that would stick a little too well through the years.

As we were growing up, Dolly and I were always together. When we were small, we would run between our grandma and grandpa's house down the road, as well as back and forth to Aunt Ruth and Uncle Ted's home.

We especially loved being at the gas station. Mom started doing the books for Dad when we were pretty young, so it became our special hang-out. We would spend hours playing hide-and-seek amongst the tires, or messing with the displays.

Archie was probably our favorite mechanic. He would tease us and make us giggle. We loved to get peanuts from the nickel machine, and he showed us how to blow softly on the peanuts and watch the red skins fly into the air.

Sometimes, Dad gave us "rides" on the hoist. That's the hydraulic lift that raised the cars up so they could be worked on from below. We would hop on top of it, and he would push the button that lifted us into the air. At the end of the night, he would spray the ground with a high powered hose to wash it, and we always seemed to end up wet in the process. It never failed to make us laugh.

On Sundays, my family went to church. I learned all the important Bible stories—even prayed a prayer to Jesus when I was young. But somehow, what I learned at church stayed at church. During the week, for the most part, we didn't really talk about God. The one thing from my childhood I wish I could have changed was to have somehow learned to integrate my faith with the real life situations I would deal with as I grew older.

When Dolly hit her early teen's, it was almost as though a switch had been activated. One moment she listened to our parents and was very obedient, and the next moment, she kind of went wild. It began when she started spending time with the party crowd at school. Studying was no longer a priority. Nights were for parties where alcohol, drugs, and boys were never in short supply.

Suddenly, I had a hard time recognizing my sweet sister. She wasn't only my sister; she was my best friend, and I missed her. There were many nights when Mom waited up for Dolly, worrying about her. Once, we were even woken up in the middle of the night by a police officer with Dolly in tow.

I, on the other hand, was the "good girl." I stayed focused on academics and other school activities. I even became the president of my youth group at church.

By the time I was in junior high, I had a problem. I was six feet tall. That definitely put a crimp in the romance department.

Unless you counted the time I chased down David Johnson during recess, I'd never kissed a boy. I had lots of male friends—best buddies, in fact. But what boy dated a girl who was several inches taller than him? That would require someone both mature as well as secure in their masculinity—which, of course, eliminated the entire male population anywhere in the near vicinity.

Consequently, I spent lots of time listening to boys talk about the girls they liked. Occasionally, I was even asked to deliver messages back and forth between the potential "love birds," when all along my heart felt sick. Why couldn't he see me? Or rather he *could* see me, and that was the problem. I wasn't who he was attracted to.

I told myself it didn't matter. I had goals and didn't need the distraction of boys. I had seen plenty of broken hearts over the years. Look at all the pain I had been able to avoid.

But deep down it hurt. Why couldn't I have been more petite? I had always had a good sense of humor—even learned to make fun of myself in order to get a laugh. But the truth was sometimes I felt like a clown on stilts.

And even clowns don't like being alone.

Compromise

I met Brian while out "cruising the loop." It was what teenagers did in a small town on a Saturday night. We would all pile into cars and drive around the downtown area, blasting our radios and yelling greetings to each other.

If you saw someone you thought was cute, you would yell out for them to meet you at the park downtown. It was our version of lover's lane, without the beautiful view.

When I saw Brian, I did a double-take. Wow. Longish dark, curly brown hair, and brown eyes, with a smile designed to melt a woman's heart. Not only that, but I could tell by how high he was sitting that unless he had really short legs, he was at least as tall as me. I couldn't let him just go by without trying. What did I have to lose?

When I yelled for him to meet me and he said "yes," my heart nearly did a summersault. What would I say to him? What would he think of me? I was about to meet a guy in the park for the first time. Outwardly I was bold, but inwardly my heart was about to jump out of my chest. He just *had* to like me.

We pulled up at the same time, and when he unfolded himself from the car my knees went weak. He wasn't much taller than I was, but that was great. Walking around the park with a tall, dark stranger holding my hand was exhilarating. I almost wanted to shake myself to be sure it wasn't a dream.

Standing beside my car, exchanging phone numbers and saying goodnight, Brian leaned down, and I lifted my face for his kiss. His lips were soft and warm, and my stomach did a little flip. I had always dreamed of this ... being able to look into someone's eyes without having to bend my neck. Someone who was hopefully attracted to me and might someday grow to love me.

Could he tell how inexperienced I was? He was different than any of the other guys I'd hung out with. There was a sophistication about him, as well as a bit of a "wild and crazy guy" attitude. He didn't seem to care much about what anyone else thought, and he made me laugh.

After that, we became a steady item, and I found myself bending to Brian's standards. I hadn't wanted to have sex before marriage, but a guy like Brian could have whoever he wanted. For some reason, he had chosen me, and I didn't want to lose him.

~

I finished high school and was in my first year of college when I noticed I'd missed at least one period. I didn't want to believe I could be pregnant. That happened to other people somewhere else, but it couldn't happen to me. Yet I began to think about how I'd been really tired for a while, and that I'd had some nausea, but just chalked it up to the flu.

I wanted to deny what was happening, but I called Brian and over dinner told him I was pretty sure I was pregnant. Without hesitation, He offered to call his sister to get the number of an abortion clinic.

That was the extent of our discussion. Why hadn't I brought up other options? If he had offered to marry me, I would have gladly. But there was no mention of marriage or babies, and that fast, the course was set.

I knew I couldn't tell my parents. They would have been so disappointed in me. They didn't even know we were having sex. No—I was the one who had taken the risk, and now I would have to face the consequences.

Abortion had only been legalized for a little over a year. Those in authority were saying it was okay, so I told myself it must be true.

The first doctor's appointment seemed to trigger a chain of events that I felt powerless to stop. It was like I was a cow in a shoot being jostled along, unknowingly going to the butcher.

I must have been given a physical exam, but I don't recall any of that. My one clear memory of our interaction was that when I said I wanted an abortion, there was no discussion or counseling of any kind. He simply wrote out a prescription for the abortion and gave it to me; essentially handing me my child's death warrant.

The morning of my abortion it was a beautiful, sunshiny day. A stark contrast to how I felt. Everything inside was a dark, swirling mass of emotions. The track was laid out in front of me, but deep down I didn't want to abort. Yet turning around felt as impossible as it would be for the cow.

When I arrived, eventually my name was called, and I was brought to a room. They told me they would have to put something in my cervix to make it open. I had no idea what they meant, but later I learned that it was called laminaria; a seaweed product that as it swells causes the cervix to dilate.

After that, I was told to go somewhere for a while and was given a second appointment several hours later. I remember Brian and me walking around a park for a long time, then sitting under a tree for quite a while.

Once I finally returned and was prepped for the procedure, the nurse offered for me to hold her hand. At first, that seemed ridiculous. But soon the pain was excruciating. I found myself gripping the woman's hand so tightly, I was surprised she didn't protest. It was as though my insides were being twisted and then torn from my body. It seemed to go on for a very long time.

The thing that haunted me for years were the broken bits of conversation between the doctor and the nurse. Something about there being "more parts."

More parts? What did that mean?

Until that moment, I had tried not to think in terms of a *baby*. It was just tissue, right? I wanted to ask them what they were talking about. But did I really want to know?

I don't recall much of anything else. If there were physical effects I no longer remember. The biggest thing I felt was the relief. Just knowing it was over, and I could finally move on.

That evening, I showed up for my shift as a waitress, telling one of my co-workers that I'd had an abortion and that it was no big deal.

Why did I say that? Hadn't it actually been a pretty *big* deal? The excruciating pain? The confusion about what had been going on? The words I was afraid to look at too closely?

Maybe I was the one who needed to believe it was no big deal. But deep down, I knew nothing would ever be the same.

Deception

After that day, I tried to move on, telling myself what I had done was okay. For a little while, I even told a few more people about the abortion, putting it in a positive light.

Things were far from "rosy" with Brian. I'd been drawn to him, because he had seemed so much wiser in the ways of the world. But eventually, I no longer admired that about him. Or much of anything else, for that matter.

Into alcohol and drugs, he partied pretty heavily. To fit in with him and his friends, sometimes I would drink and do drugs too. He was also into using me as a punching bag.

My dad had always been respectful to my mother, never raising his hand to her or to his children. The first time Brian back-handed me for something I said, it wasn't only a shock to my senses, it was a shock to my spirit. And he didn't care about whether he left marks either. It was my problem to figure out how to disguise them. I became quite creative at explaining away cuts and bruises.

Part of the reason I was always getting hit was that I couldn't seem to keep my mouth shut. I tried not to get him riled up; tried to tippy-toe around him. But some things I just couldn't let go. One time, I stood up to him for breaking our plans because he'd

225

gotten a better offer to go party with friends. Within seconds he had punched me in the mouth repeatedly. "I told you to shut up! You are so stupid! Why do you make me do that?" I staggered back, cowering with my arms up, trying to protect myself as best I could.

The next day, I came to work with my mouth and lips swollen and dark blue. One of the guys I worked with said, "You look like you sucked on a blue ink pen. Did he hit you?"

I just ducked my head, avoiding his gaze.

"That's not cool."

What had happened to the fairytale existence I hoped I would have? At six feet tall, I knew I would never be like Cinderella. The thought of a handsome prince combing the countryside in search of a girl my size to fit a tiny glass slipper was pretty comical.

Still, like any other woman, I wanted to be loved. To have someone believe I was beautiful; that I was *the one*. Clearly, Brian was not that person. So why did I find myself exchanging rings with him in front of my family and friends?

Underneath it all, I simply couldn't fathom someday having to tell a man who wanted to spend his whole life with me that I'd had an abortion. So I picked bachelor number three, even though he was the last person I wanted to be with.

Besides, I didn't deserve a "good guy" anyway.

~

Five years later, I was in a hospital bed holding a beautiful baby boy. Ten toes and ten fingers, and bright, inquisitive eyes. I was completely mesmerized and overjoyed as I witnessed the miracle of *life*.

But that was also when the truth hit me like a death blow: *I ended the life of this baby's brother or sister. My* <u>*child*</u>.

Suddenly, I found it hard to breathe. How could I have done such a thing? What had I been thinking? The truth was shattering. I had allowed someone to rip a precious life from my womb.

All along, guilt and shame had been lurking in the shadows of my mind, ready to attack. Now, in the midst of the joy and delight of holding my baby for the first time, I could no longer escape. Leaping from the shadows into harsh reality, the crushing weight of shame and self-hatred pounced, ready to consume.

For the first time, I understood I had gravely sinned against God and was in need of His forgiveness.

I tried to stuff it all in as best I could. But it was as if

I had a mortal wound across my abdomen, and needed to apply continuous pressure to prevent my "insides" from spilling out.

I cherished every moment with little Johnny, while Brian spent very little time with either one of us. The abuse continued, but thankfully he never touched our son in anger. Still, had he heard his father yelling at me? Heard me whimpering?

Whereas once I had felt so capable and strong, now I questioned myself constantly. All I heard on an almost daily basis was how stupid I was. My confidence was nearly non-existent.

One time, I was really scared and tried to call 911. Brian ripped the phone cord out of the wall and told me, "not even God can help you now."

~

Johnny was about two and a half years old when I decided to take him to the church I had gone to pretty much all my life. It felt good to be back. We never missed a Sunday after that if I could help it. Although I invited him, Brian wanted nothing to do with God.

One Sunday, there was a special speaker at church. I was shocked to hear him talking very passionately about abortion. At one point, he was nearly jumping up and down, trying to get the people in the congregation to wake up from their lethargy.

Right there in the pew, with people on all sides, I cracked wide open. It was hard not actually to begin wailing, so deep was the well of pain inside me. Even though I limited my grief to silent sobs, I wondered what the people around me thought of my behavior. But whether I liked it or not, from that point on I was never able to stop from crying during the sermon, regardless of the topic.

Johnny was still two when I had Carrie. I was thrilled to have another precious gift from God, but I worried about their safety. I had never seen Brian's aggression turned towards his children. But what if anything ever happened to me? What then?

I had thought about leaving Brian countless times, but fear had stopped me in my tracks. Deep down, I believed if he was drunk enough and angry enough he was capable of murder.

Without ever intending to help me, his decision to move out for a while and have an affair with a younger woman was exactly what I needed to gather the courage to end our marriage. And when he came back, thinking he could have both a wife and a girlfriend, that only served to solidify my decision.

Dolly was the one who helped me navigate through the divorce proceedings. It was a good thing she came to the lawyer's office with me, because I cried so hard I needed a translator just to make sense out of what I was trying to say.

It's hard to change after so many years of taking abuse. It almost becomes a way of life … a whole different mindset. Fear and pride had held me captive in that relationship for nearly ten years. Not only fear that he would do something to the children or to me if I left him, but also fear of what everyone would think if I got a divorce. I was the first one in my family to end a marriage. I didn't want anyone to know about the physical abuse I had put up with during all that time, either. It made me feel weak and stupid, just as Brian had told me repeatedly. I never thought I would be grateful for his unfaithfulness, but in a way I was.

Finally, I felt I had permission to close that chapter of my life, and to walk away for good.

Together

It had taken me years to find Brian, and to say that he hadn't been a good choice as a partner would be putting it mildly. I had pretty much resigned myself to raising my kids alone when a co-worker talked me into attending a group called "Parents without Partners." With a name like that, I should have known better.

After the official meeting, I was sitting at the bar of the restaurant when this guy came towards me. He was short and stocky, with coke bottle glasses. Wearing black pants and a white shirt, complete with a pocket protector, he definitely was *not* my type. The next thing I knew he had hoisted himself up on the bar stool beside me, and looking up, in all seriousness said, "So, what's your sign?"

That was my cue. Not only to leave the restaurant but to stop pursuing another partner period. I got home and laid it out to the Lord. If He wanted me to meet someone, then He would have to bring them to my doorstep. I didn't have the time or the inclination to weed through countless men in search of a potential husband, as well as a daddy for my young children. Singlehood sounded better by the minute.

Then one afternoon, my friend, Susan, called to ask if I could come over for dinner that night. And could I find a sitter for the kids?

That was odd because Susan adored my children. Immediately suspicious, I asked why. She explained that a friend, named Aaron, was also invited. He was a single parent raising a little girl and having a hard time meeting nice women. Could I come share a meal with them and then play some cards afterward?

She wanted to set me up on a blind date? Really? She was pretty persistent, but I nearly turned her down. However, I hadn't sought this out, and there was no commitment involved, beyond dinner. So I agreed. At least I would have some adult conversation and eat a delicious meal. Susan was an excellent cook.

When I met Aaron, I was pleasantly surprised. He was kind of cute and had a good sense of humor. The very first thing I did beyond introductions was to show off pictures of my three-year-old and six month old. I didn't want him to be under any illusions about who I was.

It was a nice enough evening, but he didn't seem particularly interested in me. He hadn't even asked for my phone number until we were outside and I was hurrying to my car. There was quite a winter storm in progress, with the snow coming down so hard that it made it difficult to even to see, let alone write down a number. Couldn't he have thought to ask for my number while we were still warm and toasty inside?

But, he more than made up for any inconvenience by calling me several times that week. It surprised me that a guy would be as open as he was about himself and about what he wanted out of life. Even about his mistakes. I discovered that he'd been a single dad for five years, ever since he went through a divorce and was awarded full custody. It was sad to hear that his daughter, Annie, had only seen her mother a couple of times in all those years. I couldn't imagine how that would make her feel.

I was fairly open with him as well. I figured what did I have to lose? By our last conversation it seemed like there wasn't anything we hadn't discussed.

I was really looking forward to our first truly official "date," but it turned out to be extremely awkward. Sitting at the restaurant table as we waited for our food, the conversation was strained at best. What was the matter? We'd talked non-stop on the phone. Now, face-to-face, we both clammed up. All in all, a pretty disastrous evening.

I don't think I would have agreed to another date, except that Dolly told me I should at least give him a second chance before completely writing him off. I had told her about our late night conversations, and I think in a small way Aaron had impressed her.

The next time Aaron and I were together things went far better, and I was truly grateful for my baby sister's advice. Somehow, this guy was starting to get to me.

A couple of weeks later, Aaron called me asking if I would mind picking up his daughter so she could go to Sunday school with Johnny and Carrie. I refused, telling him If he wanted his daughter to go to church, he could bring her himself.

I tried to act nonchalant when a little while later Aaron slipped into my pew. What surprised me, even more, was that after that he never missed a Sunday. From that day on, Aaron was by my side.

Only three months from the day we met, we were married. If anyone had told me I would be re-married only six months from my divorce, I would have told them they were insane. Somehow we just knew it was the right thing to do.

Not long after the wedding, we had a huge argument. I can't remember what it was about, but I know it was a verbal "knock down drag out" fight. The next morning, Aaron asked if I wanted a divorce. I looked at him like he'd grown two heads.

"I've already been through one divorce, and I don't plan on going through another. Murder, on the other hand, isn't out of the question."

Several months later, I got a shock. Somehow, Aaron had neglected to mention a previous marriage. It had been extremely brief, but it's not something you just forget to mention.

I was furious. Just as I was getting really worked up, I heard in my spirit, "What have *you* not told *him*?"

That took the wind right out of my sails. Who did I think I was? I had been the queen of deception for years. First the abuse, then the abortion, and back to more abuse. I had even gotten pretty good at lying to myself.

So, right then and there, I told Aaron about the abortion. I didn't hold anything back. I was tired of hiding and never wanted to do that again.

Our marriage required a lot of adjusting and compromising on both our parts, as blended families usually do. Aaron's daughter, Annie, was seven years old at the time of our wedding. I gave her the option of either calling me Mom or Sandy, but she immediately chose Mom. I'm not sure I was consciously aware that she was just about the same age as my aborted child would have been. I only knew that I was very grateful for how well Annie and my other children adapted so quickly to each other, behaving like true siblings, fights and all. For the most part, they all got along famously.

A few years later, we had a daughter together whom we named Arianna. She was a delight. What a joy to have so much life around me. No one was beating me down anymore, and our home was filled with the laughter of children and the love of their parents.

Revealed

I had known about a pregnancy center in the area and began sensing the Lord's nudge to volunteer my time there. I wanted to give others the help I wish I had received.

Finally, I signed up. As I drove there that night, I reminded myself that I would *not* even mention I was post-abortive. But when we were going around the room telling our names and what brought us there, immediately I blurted out I'd had an abortion.

Why in the world had I said that? I couldn't believe that I had done it, but in the end, it helped me process my healing that much quicker.

I also strongly resisted the idea of going through a post-abortion healing course. Wasn't coming and volunteering enough? It was called *Forgiven and Set Free*. But it turned out that taking the class was so wonderful; soon I was volunteering to help lead future classes. It seemed that every time I helped others through their journey toward healing, I found another level of healing for myself as well.

Eventually, I began to wonder when one of my children or other family members might hear about my abortion second hand. I decided I didn't want to take that risk, so one by one I met with my children and told each of them the truth about their brother or sister who was in heaven.

237

It proved to be one of the hardest things I'd ever done. They had all known how passionate I was about abortion, but not why it went so deep. In the beginning, they struggled even believing it was true.

Especially my youngest, Arianna. She told me that if she'd heard it from anyone else, she would have called them a liar and been tempted to hurt them for talking about her mom like that.

We wept many tears together, but instead of causing my children to pull away from me in revulsion, as I had believed all those years, we were drawn closer than ever before.

A few months later, I received a call from Arianna. She had been in a difficult marriage for a few years, with a husband who drank and was abusive. The apple didn't fall far from the tree, and that broke my heart. She lived about three hours away, but we still called each other a few times a week.

As we talked, she sounded a little on edge. So when she said, "I have something to tell you, but it can wait till later."

Instantly my mama radar went up. "No, tell me now." That went back and forth for a couple of minutes, which convinced me that she wanted to tell me, but was afraid to.

Finally, she started sobbing. "I'm pregnant again!

I'm so stupid! I can't have another baby so soon. I think I have to have an abortion."

Immediately, my heart squeezed, as though it were in a vise grip that was being tightened. *Not my daughter too, Lord!*

"No, you don't Arianna. You can do this." She already had two little girls just seventeen months apart, the youngest being only six months old. Yet I knew all too well what the fallout from abortion would bring.

My daughter continued to sob, so that it was hard to understand her. But when I learned that both her husband and mother-in-law were strongly pressuring her to abort, I was livid.

"Arianna, you're telling me this because you know what happened to me. Deep down you don't want to go through what I have all these years. Trust me; you can do this. Your dad and I will help you. If you need a place to stay, you can always come home."

"You're sure I can do this, Mom?"

"Yes. I'm not saying it won't be hard, but the alternative is unthinkable." Arianna had a tough exterior, but underneath was a tender heart. The toll an abortion would have taken was beyond my comprehension.

Arianna did not abort, and a few months later she

gave birth to another little girl. It wasn't easy. She ended up filing for divorce and coming to stay with Aaron and me for three months, only to stop the proceedings and return to her husband. He said he had changed and that he wouldn't hit her again. He was sober now.

It was an ugly time, and there were many sleepless nights spent alternately worrying and praying; usually a combination of both. Eventually, she left her abusive husband for good and lived with us for three years. She needed our help with the girls, as well as financially. It was quite an adjustment for Aaron and me both, but the sound of children laughing warmed my heart.

Today, Arianna has a very good job, and her own house just blocks from where the girls go to school. Her three daughters are only about two years apart, and they're very close, like three peas in a pod. They have their moments, but for the most part, they're best friends.

Sometimes I stop and marvel at God's timing. What if I hadn't told my children about my abortion? Without that knowledge, would she have ever told me about what she was strongly considering?

~

Before I went "public" with the abortion, at times I would cringe when people at church would praise me for my "good work" at the center. Sometimes they would follow the statement up with an, "I just can't understand how anyone could murder their own child!"

I would want to jump back, as though I'd just been burned. I felt like such a hypocrite. Without realizing it, they were talking about *me*. Pouring salt on an open wound. Heaping on even more shame, which before my deeper healing was still very much present. There was nothing *good* about what I was doing. I was only hoping somehow the Lord would use the sin in my life to help someone find healing on the other side of abortion, or to help another avoid the pain altogether.

Now, when someone asks me how anyone could kill their own child, I tell them how I was feeling and what I was thinking at the time of my own abortion. About the deception I was under and how dearly I have paid for that decision. I have encouraged people to see others who have experienced an abortion as the "walking wounded." Hoping their eyes would be opened to the fact that statistically there are many people in our congregation who have also had abortions, and are in need of healing. If we hurl out judgment wherever we go, how will they ever find the courage to seek help?

Later, I was approached by our newspaper to do an article about my abortion story. I felt the Lord pushing me out even further from my safety zone. I surprised myself when I said "yes." From cowering in silence to a newspaper article was a huge leap.

Aaron and I don't have a perfect marriage. Big surprise, when two flawed individuals are a part of the union. We're two stubborn people with polar opposite personalities. But we love God, and we love each other, so we work through our differences, overlooking things that after thirty plus years may never change.

Although our sense of humor is very different, I love my husband's laugh. After all, this time, I find it amazing that he still enjoys spending time with me. Whenever we can, we still enjoy long hikes and camping together. Recently, while we were out on a trail, Aaron looked over at me. "You know you're one in a million, don't you? How many other women would do this with their husbands?"

I would think many, but I might be wrong. All I know is I feel so blessed God allowed us to find each other. That my children had a stepdad who truly loved and cared for them, as though they were his own. And so they are.

I now have eight grandchildren, so our family gatherings are a happy, noisy affair. How I love to hear their laughter! I hope I'm a fun grandma, but I'm definitely not a push-over. My theory is, if you keep them busy that's the best preventative medicine.

And Dolly and I? After all these years, she's still my best friend. We live in the same town and go to the same church. Our children have grown up together, and people still can't keep their names straight. And if we haven't had enough one-on-one time, we take off on a sister's only vacation getaway.

Mom's doing as well as can be expected, with her advancing years and some dementia issues. She's in an assisted living community, and so far that's working out.

I sure miss Dad. We lost him quite suddenly several years ago when he collapsed due to a brain aneurysm. He never regained consciousness. He was only in his seventies, and still so full of life. He left a hole in our family, and I can't wait for the day when I see him again.

There's someone else I'm missing more than anyone. Years ago, I had picked a name for my aborted child during a memorial service. Not feeling certain as to whether the child was a boy or a girl, I chose Shelby for the name, thinking it could work either way.

A few years ago, Aaron and I were in Colorado, spending time with our son, Johnny. A couple of days after arriving, we were sitting in a little country café, when the front door opened up and a chorus of

"Shelby!" rang out. All eyes turned toward a tall, muscular man walking towards our table. He was about the same size as my son, sitting beside me. And somehow I knew. My aborted child was a boy. How I long to one day see his face and to hold him close!

Every day, I am astounded by God's amazing grace. I still face days when I struggle with my decision to abort all those years ago. But I praise God for the forgiveness He has extended to me, and how He has taken something so painful, even sinful, and used it to bring about much good. In God's economy, nothing is ever wasted.

I count it such an incredible honor that I get to teach children's Sunday school. To be around so much energy—so much *life*. All those bright little faces looking up at me; minds like sponges, soaking up God's word.

One of my favorite Bible verses is John 10:10, *"The thief comes only to steal and kill and destroy. I came that they would have life, and that they would have it abundantly."* I continue to be astounded at the goodness God has poured out on my behalf.

For the rest of my life, with every fiber of my being, I want to live for the One who gave His life for me. I never want to stop singing His praises to all who will listen.

"Jesus said to her, "Everyone who drinks of this water will be thirsty again, but whoever drinks of the water I will give him will never be thirsty forever. The water that I will give him will become in him a spring of water welling up to eternal life."

John 4:13-14 (ESV)

Ribbon Reflection

No one just wakes up one morning and decides, "I think I'll have an abortion today." Most little girls dream of having someone to love and babies to hold. Abortion was never a part of her "happily ever after."

No, the path to that choice happens one step at a time. Yet, much like Sandy, many feel as though a mechanism has been set in motion, and they are powerless to reverse the course. Like the proverbial cow in the shoot, once they begin down that path toward abortion, it feels impossible to turn around and go in the opposite direction.

Like everyone else, Sandy's choices started well before the day she learned she was pregnant.

She longed to have the love of a man and to have the sense they belonged with each other. But because of her height, she felt disqualified from obtaining that dream. Until she met Brian.

Early on, she saw the red flags—excessive drug and alcohol use, making sexual demands, being possessive and abusive in almost every way. Despite the fact that she had to compromise in order to remain in that relationship, she felt he was her only option. Either she compromised and had someone in her life or she held her ground and remained alone.

One of the saddest parts of Sandy's story is that she chose to marry her abusive, drug addicted partner because she couldn't imagine having to confess her abortion to another man. There was a pervasive sense that, "I made my bed, now I have to lie in it."

I can only imagine how helpless she felt... how trapped. Nothing was ever going to change, and there was no going back.

BUT GOD.

Sandy reminds me so much of the Samaritan woman who encountered Jesus at a well. The true story is found in the Bible, in John, chapter 4. She, too, must have felt trapped by her circumstances. Married five times and currently living with someone who was not her husband would have made anyone feel hopeless to break the cycle—particularly at a far more conservative point in history. She was at the end of the line, and completely out of options.

BUT GOD.

That's when she met Jesus. Such an unexpected encounter in the middle of all that sameness. She went to draw water from a well and ended up meeting the Man who would change her life forever. For the first time, she looked into the eyes of a man who actually *saw* her. Who treated her with the respect she'd most likely never experienced before. And when He offered her living water and the ability to worship God, after believing she was forever disqualified, she was *in*.

Suddenly, a woman who was doing whatever it took to *avoid* the people in the village, ran off to beg everyone she could to come back to the well and meet the Man who told her amazing things about herself. He knew her! Didn't they want to come see for themselves? To decide if He was who He claimed He was...their Messiah?

But hadn't she been hiding? Hadn't she despised those people who had ridiculed and mocked her? Yet now, after experiencing the love of Christ, hope was restored. Suddenly she believed that *all things were possible*.

Sandy's life changed in a dramatic way as well. No, not as quickly, but just as radically. The love of Christ helped her see herself through His eyes. He gave her hope in exchange for the despair she had lived with for so long. From someone once hiding, in great fear of discovery, she now freely shares about her abortion, so that others, too, can find healing.

Sandy has a glow about her. During our talks, I was struck by her overwhelming gratitude for God's forgiveness and mercy. For His amazing grace. She is astounded to find herself surrounded by children. She lives her life fully aware that she has been *redeemed*. Aware that Jesus rescued her from her past and continues to redeem her future.

In God's economy, nothing is ever wasted. Even our sin and the tragedies in our life can be used for great good when we lay them at the feet of Jesus. When we surrender the broken pieces of our lives, God puts them back together in amazing ways, bringing beauty from the ashes of our life.

How about you? If you feel like your life is in pieces, I pray that you know there is hope in Jesus Christ. Why not tell Him right now that you want to surrender it all to Him, and give Him control.

Proverbs 3:5-6 says, *"Trust in the Lord with all your heart, and do not lean on your own understanding, in all your ways acknowledge Him, and He will make your path straight." (ESV)*

It's a beautiful promise, isn't it? As scary as it may sound, to release the reins of your life to another, I promise you won't regret it. Jesus came and died in order to give you *abundant life*.

I pray that you will call out to the Lord and take that first step toward healing and wholeness today.

Going Deeper

1. Because of Sandy's height, she began to feel as though she were "less than," as boys repeatedly overlooked her as a potential girlfriend. This set her up for the decision to later compromise her values.
   a. Is there something about yourself that has made you feel "less than?"
   b. If so, how has that played out in your life? Have your negative feelings about yourself caused you to compromise in any way? Or has it made you hold back from something good because you didn't feel good enough?

2. Sandy chose to marry Brian, even after a strong pattern of abuse, because she didn't want to admit to another man she was post-abortive. Can you think of a time when you made an important decision out of fear that someone would discover your secret?

3. Because Sandy eventually told her adult children about her abortion, she knows of at least one grandchild who was not aborted because of her vulnerability.
   a. If you have an abortion or something else in your past that is holding you captive in silence, what is something you're willing to do to step out of hiding?
   b. The lies inside our head say if we tell anyone about our shameful secret, they will hate us. After reading *Ribbon of Redemption,*

what do you think the truth is about
breaking the silence?

c. What are some of the positive outcomes
you can think of that could happen as a
result of your seeking healing from a past
abortion or another deep wound?

Dear ones,

Thank you for taking the time to read *Ribbon of Redemption*. My prayer is that you have found encouragement and hope between these pages.

If you have experienced an abortion or have been deeply affected by someone else's abortion, take courage. Healing is a process, so don't give up. Jesus came to minister to those with broken hearts. He wants to set captives free. I pray that you will be able to draw near to Him and find the strength and comfort you need.

The following page has several websites, hotlines, and resources, which you may find helpful as you seek to heal. Obviously, you won't use them all, so I am praying that you will find just the right fit for you.

I don't believe it is by accident that you found this book. If you have sensed God speaking to you, I pray you will say "yes" to His call and open the door of your heart. His arms are open wide.

Also, I would love to hear from you! Message me at jenny@jennyafarrell.com or visit my website at jennyafarrell.com.

In His love,

Jenny

Where do I go from here?

<u>Websites</u>:

abortionchangesyou.com

Care-Net.org/i-had-an-abortion

HopeAfterAbortion.com

jennyafarrell.com

silentnomoreawareness.org

wellspringsoffreedom.com

<u>Books and Group Recovery Studies</u>:

Forbidden Grief: The Unspoken Pain of Abortion, by Dr. Theresa Burke

Forgiven and Set Free: A Post-Abortion Bible Study for Women, by Linda Cochrane

Her Choice to Heal: Finding Spiritual and Emotional Healing Peace after Abortion, by Sydna Massey

Living in Color: The Goal of Post-Abortion Healing, by Sydna Massey

Hotlines:

Grief to Grace   610-203-2002

National Domestic Violence 1-800-799-SAFE

Rachel's Vineyard   1-877-HOPE4YOU

Suicide Hotline   1-800-SUICIDE

Want to Know Jesus?   1-800-NEEDHIM

About the Author

Jenny is excited about beginning to work on the second book in the *Ribbon of Redemption* series. This next collection of true stories will focus on navigating the heartbreak of grief and loss.

As a former nurse manager of a life-affirming pregnancy center, Jenny brings a fresh perspective to events uplifting life. She is also passionate about seeing women set free from whatever is holding them back. She speaks from the heart and loves connecting with her audience at both conferences and retreats. For a complete listing of topics available, you can visit her website at jennyafarrell.com.

Jenny is a pastor's wife and founder of Cottage Hope Ministries. She currently lives in Iowa with her husband of thirty-seven years. She has two adult children and three grandchildren. Jenny deeply appreciates music as the language of the soul. Whenever she is near the coast, she delights in strolling along the ocean's shore in search of shells, stones, and sea glass.

Made in the USA
Charleston, SC
15 November 2016